COOKBOOK FOR THE NEW AGE
EARTH WATER FIRE AIR

D1378812

by
BARBARA FRIEDLANDER

Photographed by
BOB CATO

Designed by IRA FRIEDLANDER

Collier Books
A Division of Macmillan Publishing Co., Inc.
NEW YORK

Collier Macmillan Publishers
LONDON

Macmillan Publishing
Co., Inc.
866 Third Avenue
New York, N.Y. 10022
Collier-Macmillan
Canada Ltd.,
Toronto, Ontario

Earth, Water, Fire, Air
is also published
in a hardcover edition
by Macmillan Publishing
Co., Inc.

Library of Congress
Catalog Card Number:
70-183860

First Collier Books
Edition 1972

Third
Printing 1973

Printed in the
United States of
America

ACKNOWLEDGMENTS

I want to thank the many people who have
been helpful in the creation of this book.
Special thanks is extended for the invaluable
assistance of Elaine Chaback and my mother,
Jessie Bankoff, and for the support and
patience of my husband, Ira.

Contents

KNEAD LOVE INTO THE BREAD YOU BAKE

INTRODUCTION

There was once a man who was hungry, and in order to appease his hunger he sat down at a certain place, closed his eyes and began to eat imaginary curry. After a while he was seen with his mouth open, endeavoring to cool his burnt tongue. Somebody asked him what the matter was. He said that in his food there was a very hot chili. The name is cool, but the thing itself is very hot. Thereupon the bystander remarked, "Oh, poor fellow, if you live on imaginary food, then why not select something far sweeter than hot chili pepper? As it is your own creation, your own doing, your own imagination, why did you not make a better choice?"

This book contains a better choice; with it, your creation, your imagination and your own doing, you can prepare wholesome as well as delicious meals. The change accompanying the New Age is affecting us in many ways. One of them is a greater awareness of the food we eat. Fresh food, simply prepared, is becoming more appealing and important. We are beginning to question the value of "convenience" foods. Not everyone can—or even wants to—go "back to nature"; but faced with the choice, wouldn't you prefer eating the naturally grown apple—undersized as it might be—to its perfectly coiffed counterpart—overfertilized, sprayed and possibly even waxed? There are alternatives.

Earth, Water, Fire, Air is more a "way-of-life book" than the kind of cookbook you are used to consulting. We offer this book to all your five senses. By using it in this way it is hoped that the sixth sense, the sense of awareness, may be tapped.

This book is intended for anyone, vegetarian or not, who might want to experience the possibilities of meals without meat, fish or fowl—without additives or preservatives. And because the emphasis is a bit different from that in other cookbooks, you will find some chapters, such as the one on grains, "heavier" than others, such as the one on dessert.

There is nothing mystical or frightening about a vegetarian meal. Abandon your concept of "the entrée" and just cook dishes that seem to go well together. Try to be aware of balance: just as you would not have a meal consisting wholly of eggs, fish and meat, so you should try to avoid too many of one kind of vegetable at the same meal. A plate of green beans, spinach and Brussels sprouts is both montonous and unwholesome. Balance proteins and carbohydrates; for example, dried beans—particularly lentils— are high in protein and combine well with rice and green salads. There are some guides to menu planning at the bottom of many recipes and on page 189.

A noticeable difference in vegetarian cooking is that the food may take a bit longer to prepare. But once you get the knack of planning and producing these kinds of dishes, you will not even notice that you are spending any extra time in the kitchen. The joy of creating such delicious, filling and healthy meals will more than compensate.

A cook can be an artist on the plate as well as at the stove. Think about color and texture when combining foods. For instance, the rich green of watercress or parsley offsets brown rice beautifully; the smoothness of a brown sauce complements crunchy wheat berry or kasha.

Most important, do not feel bound by rules. Just let your instincts and your heart run free. And above all, be happy and relaxed in the kitchen: love what you're doing and whom you're doing it for. Remember, food is very sensitive to your vibrations.

Below are brief descriptions of some of the ingredients called for in the recipes. These items can usually be purchased at natural food and department stores. I recommend using them whenever possible, although they are not essential to any recipe.

SUGAR—Raw, unrefined (a trifle less sweet than white sugar).
HONEY—Pure, raw, unfiltered.
FLOUR—Stone-ground, unfumigated. Those most commonly used are wholewheat, soy, corn—either alone or in combination.
MOLASSES—Unsulfured and pure.
MEAL—Often used interchangeably or combined with flour. Those most commonly used are sunflower, cornmeal, wheat germ.
DAIRY PRODUCTS—Natural (unprocessed) and without preservatives. You can make your own yoghurt (see page 182).
EGGS—From organically fed hens; fresh, untreated, fertilized.
OILS (and related products such as margarine, mayonnaise, etc.)—

Cold-pressed, not hydrogenated, and pure. Those most commonly used are corn, cottonseed, olive, peanut, safflower, sesame, sunflower, soy.

SALT—Sea salt (made from evaporated sea water), vegetable salt. Note: yeast flavorings such as Marmite may be substituted for salt.

NUTS—Raw, without salt or oil. Nuts are an excellent source of protein. For cooking they are best toasted first.

SEEDS—Whole, unfumigated. Sesame seeds in particular are an excellent source of protein.

MARGARINE—May be substituted for butter in any recipe. See OILS for recommended type of margarine.

TAMARI SAUCE—Pure soy sauce made from soy beans, water, wholewheat flour and sea salt, aged at least eighteen months. It is high in protein concentrates and a "must" in a vegetarian diet.

SPROUTS—Grown from whole and untreated seeds, beans or peas. Sprouts are very rich in vitamins (particularly B-complex) and can be eaten raw or cooked. Those most commonly used are alfalfa, soybean, mung bean.

GRAIN CEREAL—Cereal with many uses (often interchangeable with flour) made from rolled oats and seeds, nuts, and sometimes fruit. There's a recipe for making it from scratch (see page 184), or it can be purchased under various brand names.

DRIED FRUITS—Raw, unfumigated, unsulfured and sun-dried.

RICE AND GRAINS—See page 113.

MISO—Paste made by fermenting soybeans, wholewheat and sea salt for at least three years. Tamari sauce is a by-product of miso.

TAHINI—Paste made from hulled sesame seeds; also known as sesame butter.

VEGETABLES AND FRUIT—Whenever possible should be organically grown (on composted soil) and unsprayed. For these recipes, all vegetables and fruit should be well scrubbed and unpeeled (unless otherwise specified). For more information on vegetables see page 79.

Here is a brief list of equipment that is particularly useful for many of the recipes in this book:

1. Electric blender (preferably with different speeds for blending, puréeing, chopping, etc.), or food mill.

2. Vegetable steamer. There is a fairly elaborate (expensive) pot made just for this purpose, but I have found steaming easy, quick, and successful by using a small folding steel steamer that is like a strainer with legs and sits in any large pan. (See page 79 for procedure.)

3. All pots and pans referred to are heavy, made of stainless steel, iron, or stoneware. (No aluminum, please!)

4. A chopper/slicer, mechanical or electric, for fruits and vegetables is a very handy time-saving device.

5. A mortar and pestle are essential for grinding seeds, herbs and spices (unless you have an electric nut and seed grinder).

A GLOSSARY OF VEGETABLES

ARTICHOKES

Preparation: Use whole, hearts and/or bottoms.
Cooking methods: Bake, steam,* deep-fry hearts dipped in batter.
Serve hot with sauces, with butter, with lemon, stuffed.
Serve chilled (pre-cooked) marinated, in salads, in sandwiches with dressings, stuffed.

ASPARAGUS

Preparation: Use whole (bottom of stalks removed) or tops only; chop.
Cooking methods: Bake, steam, quick-sauté.*
Serve hot with sauces, with butter, with toasted almonds, baked au gratin.
Serve chilled (pre-cooked) in salads, marinated, with sauces, with dressings, in sandwiches.
Serve raw in salads.

AVOCADOS

Preparation: Cut in half, peel, slice or chop.
Serve raw in salads, in sandwiches, as an appetizer, au vinaigrette, puréed in hot or cold soups and sauces.

BEETS

Preparation: Use whole with or without stems and tops; slice, chop, grate.
Cooking methods: Steam, boil in soups, bake, deep-fry in batter.
Serve hot with lemon or cream sauce, with butter, in soup (borscht).
Serve chilled (pre-cooked) pickled (with onions), in salads, as an appetizer, in soup (borscht) with sour cream, in preserves.
Serve raw grated in salads (combined with apple or watercress or horseradish).

* See page 79 for procedure.

BROCCOLI

Preparation: Use whole (bottom of stalks removed) or flowerlets.
Cooking methods: Steam, quick-sauté, deep-fry in batter.
Serve hot with melted cheese or Hollandaise sauce, baked au gratin, with yoghurt and wheat germ or chopped nuts, in casseroles, in combination with other vegetables.
Serve chilled (pre-cooked) in salads, in sandwiches, with dressing.
Serve raw as an appetizer, in salads.

BRUSSELS SPROUTS

Preparation: Use whole.
Cooking methods: See BROCCOLI.
Serve hot with chestnuts or water chestnuts; see also BROCCOLI.
Serve chilled (pre-cooked): See BROCCOLI.

CABBAGE

Preparation: Use whole (leaves only): cut in large chunks, shred, chop.
Cooking methods: Steam, quick-sauté, sauté in sauces.
Serve hot with sauces, with apples and/or chestnuts (red cabbage), with noodles, in combination with other vegetables, pickled as sauerkraut, with caraway seeds, stuffed (leaves).
Serve raw juiced, in salads, as cole slaw, pickled as sauerkraut.

CARROTS

Preparation: Use whole; slice, grate, curl.
Cooking methods: Steam, quick-sauté, bake by itself or in breads, cakes or cookies, boil in soups, stews or sauces.
Serve hot with butter and/or honey, with sauces, baked au gratin, puréed or whole in soups, with toasted sesame seeds or nuts, in soufflés or custards.

Serve chilled (pre-cooked) in salads, in preserves.
Serve raw juiced, in combination with other vegetables, in salads, in cole slaw, as an appetizer, in ice cream.
Note: Can be grated in tortes and sautéed in breads.

CAULIFLOWER   See BROCCOLI

Note: Also can be stuffed whole and baked.

CELERY

Preparation: Use whole; slice, chop, grate.
Cooking methods: Steam, quick-sauté, braise, boil in soups, stews or sauces.
Serve hot with sauces, in combination with other vegetables, in casseroles, in soups, in stuffings and fillings, in sauces.
Serve chilled (pre-cooked) with cream sauce.
Serve raw juiced, in salads, in sandwich spreads, plain or stuffed as an appetizer.

CHESTNUTS

Preparation: Use whole or chop.
Cooking methods: Blanch and boil, steam, roast, quick-sauté.
Serve hot in sauces, in combination with other vegetables (particularly cabbage and green beans), puréed in soufflés, in casseroles and stuffings.
Serve chilled (pre-cooked) puréed in puddings and desserts.
Note: Cooked and puréed chestnuts may also be baked in tortes or used as pie fillings.

CHICORY

Preparation: Use whole or torn leaves.
Cooking methods: Steam, braise.
Serve hot with sauces, in combination with other vegetables.
Serve raw in salads (combined with other greens), as a garnish.

CORN

Preparation: Use on cob or kernels alone.
Cooking methods: Steam, boil in soups, stews or sauces, bake.
Serve hot with butter, with sauces, in combination with other vegetables, in casseroles, in puddings, in soups, in fritters.
Note: Raw corn can be ground into meal.

CUCUMBER

Preparation: Slice, chop.
Cooking methods: Steam, boil in soups.
Serve hot with sauce as omelette or pancake filling.
Serve chilled (pre-cooked) puréed in soups.
Serve raw in salads, puréed in soups, in sandwiches and sandwich spreads, pickled, as an appetizer, as a garnish.

DANDELION GREENS

Preparation: Use whole; chop.
Cooking methods: Steam, quick-sauté.
Serve hot with tamari or other sauce.
Serve chilled (pre-cooked) in combination with other vegetables.
Serve raw juiced (combined with celery and carrots), in salads, as a garnish.

EGGPLANT

Preparation: Use whole; cut in half, slice, chop.
Cooking methods: Steam, quick-sauté, boil in stews, deep-fry breaded or in batter, bake.
Serve hot stuffed and baked, baked au gratin or à la parmigiana, in casseroles, combined with other vegetables, puréed in soufflés, with sauces, in stews, mashed.
Serve chilled (pre-cooked) marinated or plain in salads, chopped or mashed as an appetizer.

ENDIVE

Preparation: Use whole (leaves only); slice or chop.

Cooking methods: Steam, braise, bake, quick-sauté.
Serve hot in casseroles, with sauces, in combination with other vegetables, with nuts, in fillings.
Serve raw in salads, in sandwich spreads, in aspics, stuffed.

ESCAROLE   See CHICORY

Note: Also can be cooked in soups.

FENNEL   See CELERY

GREEN BEANS

Preparation: Use whole; snap, slice, chop.
Cooking methods: Steam, boil in soups and stews, quick sauté.
Serve hot with butter, sauces, sautéed with sunflower seeds, deep-fried in batter, whole or puréed in soups, in casseroles, in combination with other vegetables.
Serve chilled (pre-cooked) in salads.
Serve raw in salads.

JERUSALEM ARTICHOKES

Preparation: Use whole or slice.
Cooking methods: Steam, bake, quick-sauté, fry.
Serve hot with butter, with sauces, baked au gratin, in soufflés, in soups, mashed.
Serve chilled (pre-cooked) in salads.
Serve raw in salads.

KALE   See SWISS CHARD

KOHLRABI

Preparation: Use whole with or without leaves; slice, chop, grate.
Cooking methods: Steam, quick-sauté, bake, boil in soups.
Serve hot with butter, with sauces, in soups, stuffed and baked.
Serve chilled (pre-cooked) in salads.
Serve raw in salads.

LEEKS

Preparation: Use white and green parts or white only; chop or slice.
Cooking methods: Steam, boil in soups, braise, quick-sauté.
Serve hot with butter, with sauces, in casseroles, baked au gratin, in soups (usually with potatoes), in custard as pie filling.
Serve chilled (pre-cooked) marinated or plain in salads (combines well with black olives), puréed in soups (vichyssoise).

LETTUCE

Preparation: Use whole or torn leaves; chop.
Cooking methods: Steam, quick-sauté.
Serve hot with sauces, baked au gratin, stuffed and baked, in combination with other vegetables, in fillings.
Serve raw with appetizers, in salads and sandwiches.

LIMA BEANS (GREEN)

Preparation: Shell.
Cooking methods: Steam, bake, boil in soups and stews.
Serve hot with butter, with sauces, baked au gratin, in casseroles, stews and soups, in combination with other vegetables.

MUSHROOMS

Preparation: Use whole or caps only; slice or chop.
Cooking methods: Quick-sauté, sauté, steam, boil in soups, sauces and stews, grill, broil, bake, deep-fry in batter.
Serve hot in or with sauces, with butter, in casseroles, soups and stews, in combination with rice, pasta or other vegetables (particularly onions), in soufflés, stuffed or in fillings or stuffings.
Serve chilled (pre-cooked) in appetizers, salads and sandwiches, puréed in pâté, as an appetizer.

Serve raw plain or marinated in salads and appetizers.

OKRA

Preparation: Use whole (stems removed) or chop.
Cooking methods: Steam, boil in stews and soups, quick-sauté.
Serve hot with sauces, in soups and stews, in casseroles, in combination with other vegetables (particularly tomatoes).
Note: Okra powder is used as a thickener for soups and sauces. Okra slices may be strung and dried for use as a spice in stews and soups.

ONIONS

Preparation: Use whole; slice, chop, grate.
Cooking methods: Quick-sauté, sauté, steam, boil in soups, stews and sauces, braise, bake, broil, fry, deep-fry in batter.
Serve hot with butter, in or with sauces, in casseroles, in stews and soups, stuffed, in fillings or stuffings, in pancakes, in combination with other vegetables.
Serve chilled (pre-cooked) in appetizers and sandwiches, puréed in pâté.
Serve raw plain or marinated in salads and appetizers, in sandwiches, as a garnish.
Note: Onion powder or onion salt is used as a seasoning.

PARSNIPS

Preparation: Remove leaves; slice, chop, grate.
Cooking methods: Steam, quick-sauté, deep-fry, boil in soups and stews.
Serve hot with butter, with sauces, mashed with other vegetables (particularly potatoes).
Serve chilled (pre-cooked) in salads.
Serve raw grated in mayonnaise, in salads.

PEAS (GREEN)

Preparation: Shell.
Cooking methods: Steam, quick-sauté, boil

in soups, stews, and sauces, bake.
Serve hot with butter, with sauces, in pastry shells, in casseroles, puréed in soufflés, whole or puréed in soups, in combination with other vegetables (particularly onions).
Serve chilled (pre-cooked) in salads and appetizers.
Serve raw in salads.

PEPPERS (SWEET GREEN)

Preparation: Use whole; cut in quarters, slice, chop.
Cooking methods: Steam, quick-sauté, sauté, fry, deep-fry in batter, boil in stews and sauces, bake, broil.
Serve hot with sauces, stuffed and baked, in casseroles, in stews and sauces, fried, in stuffings or fillings, in combination with other vegetables, pasta or rice.
Serve chilled (pre-cooked) in salads, appetizers, and sandwich spreads.
Serve raw in salads, sandwiches, and appetizers, as an appetizer (stuffed).

PIMIENTOS   See PEPPERS

POTATOES (WHITE AND SWEET)

Preparation: Use whole; cut in quarters, slice, chop, grate.
Cooking methods: Steam, boil, sauté, fry, deep-fry alone, in batter or in pancakes, bake, roast.
Serve hot with butter, with sauces, mashed, in combination with other vegetables, baked (plain or stuffed), as dumplings or pancakes, in puddings, in casseroles, soups, stuffings and stews, mashed and fried.
Serve chilled (pre-cooked) as a salad.
Note: Cooked and puréed potatoes may be baked with flour into rolls and bread.

PUMPKINS   See SQUASH

Note: Also can be mashed and baked in pie.

RADISHES

Preparation: Use whole; slice, chop, grate.

Serve raw juiced (combined with celery), in salads, as appetizers (black radishes, grated), in sandwiches.

SORREL   See WATERCRESS

SPINACH

Preparation: Use whole leaves and stems or leaves only; tear or chop.
Cooking methods: Steam, quick-sauté, deep-fry in batter, boil in soups.
Serve hot with butter, with sauces, puréed in soufflés and puddings, baked au gratin, in pies and casseroles, in combination with other vegetables, pasta or rice, in fillings, soups, and dumplings.
Serve raw juiced (combined with carrots and celery), in salads, plain or marinated, in mayonnaise.

SQUASH (YELLOW, BUTTERNUT, WINTER, ACORN)

Preparation: Use whole; slice, chop, grate.
Cooking methods: Steam, quick-sauté, bake, boil in soups and stews, broil.
Serve hot with butter, with sauces, in stews, and casseroles, sliced or puréed in soups, stuffed and baked, in combination with other vegetables, dried beans, rice or pasta, mashed.
Serve chilled (pre-cooked) in salads, as an appetizer, puréed in custards.
Serve raw in salads and appetizers, mixed with cream cheese in sandwich spreads.

SWISS CHARD

Preparation: Use leaves and stems; chop.
Cooking methods: Quick-sauté, steam, boil in soups.
Serve hot with butter, with sauces, in soups, in combination with other vegetables.

TOMATOES

Preparation: Use whole; slice or chop.
Cooking methods: Steam, quick-sauté, grill, broil, bake, boil in soups, stews and sauces.
Serve hot with sauces, stuffed and baked, in stuffings and fillings, in casseroles, soups, stews and sauces, puréed in soufflés, in combination with other vegetables, pasta or rice.
Serve chilled (pre-cooked) in appetizers, marinated, stuffed.
Serve raw juiced, in salads, marinated, stuffed, in sandwiches and appetizers.

TURNIPS

Preparation: Use whole with or without leaves; slice or grate.
Cooking methods: Steam, quick-sauté, bake, fry, boil in soups and stews.
Serve hot with butter, with sauces, in soups and stews, stuffed and baked, deep-fried in batter, mashed, in combination with other vegetables (particularly potatoes).

WATERCRESS

Preparation: Use whole leaves and stems or leaves only; chop.
Cooking methods: Steam, quick-sauté, boil in soups, bake.
Serve hot with sauces, in combination with other vegetables, puréed in hot or cold soups.
Serve raw juiced (combined with carrots and celery), in salads, in appetizers, in sandwiches and sandwich spreads, as a garnish.

ZUCCHINI

Preparation: Use whole; slice, chop, grate.
Cooking methods: Steam, quick-sauté, deep-fry breaded or in batter, broil, bake.
Serve hot with sauces, stuffed and baked, in casseroles, in combination with other vegetables, in fillings, baked or broiled au gratin.
Serve chilled (pre-cooked) as an appetizer, in salads and appetizers.
Serve raw in salads.

A GLOSSARY OF HERBS

Herbs can perform magic with so many foods. They add special substance to vegetarian cooking. Experimentation is the key word—the flavors you can create are virtually limitless, and the guide below should be used merely as a starting point. Herbs can be blended together and added to food in two ways: mixed directly in; or tied together (in a cloth bag if dried herbs are being used), immersed during cooking and removed before serving.

Most herbs can be purchased in stores if you do not have the space nor the inclination to grow them. You may be able to buy some fresh, in season, but often they will be dried and packed. Buy in small quantities —once dried, they tend to lose flavor quickly. As dried herbs are more concentrated, use ½ to ¼ of the quantity for fresh herbs. *One word of advice:* No more than two courses of any one meal should be flavored with herbs.

Growing herbs from seed is very simple and enjoyable. A few feet of garden or a shelf (in a sunny place) to hold eight or ten small pots is all you need. Indoors, these herbs can be planted at any time: dill, chives, basil, parsley, marjoram, thyme, sage, oregano, mint. When grown, the herbs may be cut and used as needed, or dried and stored. Cutting often encourages growth, and your indoor herb garden may serve you year-round. Some companies now distribute indoor herb gardens complete with pots, seeds and directions.

For an outdoor garden, either plant seeds or transplant seedlings (sown indoors) in the spring.

A list of the most commonly used herbs follows. Planting instructions are given for those that are easy to cultivate.

BASIL

Use in: Cheese spreads, soups, tomato dishes, eggs, cheese soufflés, beans, eggplant, onions, peas, squash, stuffings, salads, aspics.
Planting instructions: This is an annual and should be planted in early spring in a sunny place. Cut frequently when full grown.

BAY LEAVES

Use in: Soups, eggs, sauces, beets, carrots, potatoes, stewed tomatoes, custards.

CHERVIL

Use in: Avocado and cheese spreads, soups, garnish for soups, all vegetable salads, butter and cream sauces, eggs, beets, eggplant, peas, potatoes, spinach, tomatoes; add to melted butter for vegetables.

CHIVES

Use interchangeably with onions; chives are milder.
Planting instructions: Grow in window-box. Cut often.

DILL WEED

Use in: Pickling, cheese dips and spreads, stuffed eggs, salad dressing, salads, soups, beets, spinach, broccoli, Brussels sprouts, sauerkraut, beans, turnips, potatoes.
Planting instructions: This is an annual and should be planted in the spring in a sunny place.

GARLIC

Use in: Everything as desired. Also obtainable dehydrated as a powder and in salt.

MARJORAM

Use in: Cheese dips and spreads, eggs, soups, mixed green salads, fruit salads, sauces, stuffings, Brussels sprouts, squash, peas, spinach, carrots, zucchini, kale, fruit juices.
Planting instructions: This is a perennial and should be planted in the spring in southern climates; elsewhere, it should be sown indoors and transplanted in the spring. Cut off and dry entire flower when it appears.

OREGANO

Use in: Mushrooms, avocado dips, cheese spreads, juices, salads, soups, sauces (particularly in Italian-style dishes), eggs, broccoli, lentils, mushrooms, onions, tomatoes, cabbage.
Planting instructions: Plant in the spring in a sunny place.

PARSLEY

Use in: Cheese and avocado dips and spreads, garnish for soups, sauces, eggs, salads; cook in vegetable soups, stews;

juice (combined with carrots and celery).
Planting instructions: This is a biennial and should be planted in the spring.

PEPPERMINT

Use in: Beverages, juices, tea, garnish for fruit salads and desserts, bean and pea soups, sauces, fruit and yoghurt dressing, vegetable, Waldorf and cole slaw salads, cream cheese, carrots, peas, potatoes, spinach, zucchini.
Planting instructions: Plant in rich, moist soil in the spring. It is a perennial and grows like a weed; it should be controlled.

ROSEMARY

Use in: Fruit salads, jam, beverages, soups (particularly in pea, potato, and spinach soups), sauces, eggs, cauliflower, cucumber, mushrooms, peas, potatoes, spinach, and green salads.
Planting instructions: A perennial; transplant seedlings in spring to a dry sunny place.

SAFFRON

Use in: Butter, eggs, cream cheese, squash, zucchini, rice (paella), frostings, fruit juices, sweet buns, cakes.

SAGE

Use in: Sharp cheese spreads, butter and cheese sauces, cottage cheese, creamed eggs and soufflés, carrots, eggplant, lima beans, onions, peas, tomatoes, soups.

Planting instructions: This is a perennial and should be planted in the spring in sandy or dry soil.

SUMMER SAVORY

Use in: Cheese spreads, eggs, tomato and vegetable juices, soups, salads, sauces, horseradish, artichokes, asparagus, beans, lentils, rice, sauerkraut, stewed pears.
Planting instructions: This is an annual and should be planted in the spring in a sunny place. Thin to 6 inches apart. When the flowers appear, cut and dry the entire plant.

TARRAGON

Use in: Cheese spreads, cottage cheese, juices, soups, green salads, eggs, cole slaw, fruit, sauces and salad dressings, celery, mushrooms, potatoes, spinach, tomatoes.
Planting instructions: This is a perennial. Plant only from cuttings in the spring in a fairly shady spot. Protect plants in the fall.

THYME

Use in: Borscht (beet soup), soups, aspics, beet and tomato salads, cole slaw, sauces, cottage cheese, eggs, asparagus, beans, beets, carrots, onions, zucchini, mushrooms, custards, fruit compotes, vegetable and tomato juices.
Planting instructions: This is a perennial and should be planted in a dry sunny spot in the spring.

chapter 1 SALADS

Raw vegetables and fruits should be part of everyone's daily diet. Salads provide a delicious health boost and, when served at the beginning of the meal, stimulate the appetite and aid the digestion.

Salad vegetables and fruits should be as fresh and crisp as possible. Keep greens refrigerated in tightly closed containers or plastic bags until ready to use. Then wash and dry thoroughly. Prepare salad ingredients at the last minute to retain their vitamins.

Unless otherwise specified, dressings should be added just before serving. Do not drown salads. A good rule is to use *less* dressing than is required if you are in doubt.

Wooden salad bowls should not be washed —just wipe them clean.

You will be surprised at how creative saladmaking can be. For instance, try adding cooked, leftover vegetables such as parsnips; or something unique like raw asparagus or dandelion leaves. I hope the following recipes will whet your appetite for putting together a great variety of possible salads.

MEDITERRANEAN SALAD

servings: 4   preparation time: 10 minutes

1 large head romaine lettuce (see NOTE on page 32)
2 scallions or green onions, chopped fine
1 orange, thinly sliced horizontally
½ cup black olives, pitted and sliced
½ cup hard cheese, cubed
1 tablespoon each sage and basil
4 hard-cooked eggs, chilled and sliced in half lengthwise

1. Combine all ingredients, adding eggs last.
2. Toss well with Mayonnaise Dressing (see page 166). Serve chilled.

Have You Read TRIPURA RAHASYA (THE MYSTERY BEYOND THE TRINITY) (tr.) by Sri Munagala S. Venkataramaiah?

EXOTIC GREEN WALNUT SALAD

servings: 6–8
preparation time: at least 1½ hours

1 pound green walnuts*
1 bottle white grape juice
1 shallot, diced fine
pepper to taste

1. Remove skins and cut walnuts in half.
2. Place in a bowl and cover with grape
   juice, shallot, and pepper.
3. Allow to stand in a cool place and marinate
   for one hour or longer.
4. Serve cool on bed of lettuce and
   orange slices.

*Available in specialty and gourmet food
shops.

STUFFED TOMATOES

servings: 4
preparation time: at least 1½ hours

4 large tomatoes
salt to taste
2 bunches parsley, pounded fine
2 tablespoons olive oil
4 garlic cloves, pressed

1. Cut tops off tomatoes, scoop out centers,
   and salt the insides. Turn upside down
   to drain thoroughly.
2. Combine parsley, olive oil, and garlic.
3. Divide parsley mixture into four equal parts
   and fill tomatoes. Allow to stand in a cool
   place for one hour or longer. Serve chilled
   on lettuce leaves.

CUCUMBER AND YOGHURT SALAD

servings: 4   preparation time: 1½ hours

    2 large cucumbers, sliced very thin
    2 cups yoghurt
1½ teaspoons turmeric
    2 tablespoons chopped fresh mint
      or 1 tablespoon dried mint

1. Place cucumber slices in a deep bowl.
2. Separately, blend yoghurt, turmeric, and
   mint together.
3. Pour over cucumber and toss very well.
4. Chill for at least one hour. Dressing should
   be pale green. Serve very cold.

NOTE

This salad is a delicious accompaniment to
bean dishes and curried dishes.

GRAPEFRUIT AND AVOCADO SALAD

servings: 4   preparation time: 10 minutes

2 grapefruits, peeled, sectioned, and cut
2 avocados, peeled and sliced

DRESSING:
½ cup olive oil
juice of 1 lemon
salt and pepper to taste
1 tablespoon light sweet cream (optional)
sugar (optional)

1. Mix grapefruit sections and avocado slices
   together.
2. Blend dressing. Toss well and serve
   chilled.

VARIATION

In place of lemon-oil dressing, substitute
chilled Miso and Tahini Sauce (see page 169).

ARTICHOKE AND EGG IN MAYONNAISE

servings: 2   preparation time: 5 minutes

1 large artichoke, cooked and chilled
2 tablespoons mayonnaise
2 hard-cooked eggs, chilled
2 tablespoons chopped fresh dill or parsley
2 slices pimiento

1. Divide artichoke in half and fill each half
   with 1 tablespoon mayonnaise.
2. Slice eggs and cover each artichoke half
   with egg slices. Top with herb and pimiento
   slice. Serve chilled on a bed of lettuce.

TOMATO, SCALLIONS, AND AVOCADO SALAD

servings: 4   preparation time: 1½ hours

6 tomatoes
4 scallions, diced
1 teaspoon sugar
pinch of salt
1 avocado, sliced

DRESSING
  1 teaspoon lemon juice
  1 tablespoon olive oil
½ teaspoon salt
pinch each of dry mustard and pepper
  1 teaspoon chopped chervil

1. Dip tomatoes in boiling water, remove quickly, and peel off skins. Slice thickly.
2. Place scallions in bottom of a dish. Add tomato slices, sugar, and salt. Allow to stand in a cool place for at least one hour.
3. When ready to serve, blend dressing ingredients; add avocado and toss well with dressing. Serve chilled.

MANY-VEGETABLES SALAD

servings: 4   preparation time: 10 minutes

1 large head romaine lettuce
1 cauliflower, broken into flowerlets
2 scallions, sliced
6 cooked artichoke hearts, sliced in half
6 radishes, sliced thin
1 cup cooked chick peas
handful of alfalfa sprouts
handful of toasted sesame seeds
2 pimientos, sliced thin
2 tomatoes, sliced thin

1. Tear—do not cut—lettuce into small
   pieces.
2. Combine with all other ingredients, adding
   tomatoes last.
3. Toss well with French Dressing (see
   page 166). Dressing should lightly cover—
   not drown—salad. Serve immediately.

NOTE

Lettuce is best when dry and crisp. If too
wet, put individual leaves in a tightly closed
plastic bag and place in the freezer for a few
minutes just before preparation.

MIXED-FRUIT SALAD

servings: 4   preparation time: 25 minutes

1 melon,* cubed or scooped small
1 cup strawberries, stems removed and
   cut in half
2 oranges, peeled and sliced horizontally
2 apples or pears, sliced
1 banana, sliced

DRESSING
  2 tablespoons tahini (sesame butter)
  2 tablespoons honey
  4 tablespoons yoghurt
¼ cup chopped toasted almonds
¼ cup currants
juice of ½ lemon (optional)

1. Combine all fruits in a bowl.
2. Blend dressing well and toss with fruits.
   Allow to stand at least 15 minutes before
   serving.

*Any melon in season (except watermelon)
may be used.

VARIATION

Other fruits in season can be combined
beautifully. For instance, substitute another
berry (such as blueberries) for strawberries;
peaches for melon. The only "rule" is that
there should be at least one citrus fruit and
one hard fruit (apple or pear). The rest is
up to you!

chapter 2 SOUPS

Soups are so versatile! A good soup can get a meal off to a great start—or it can be a meal in itself. When cooking soup, be generous with herbs; also, use the outer leaves of vegetables like carrots, celery, and cabbage (and discards from salad greens). Soups benefit greatly from the use of leftover vegetables, appropriate sauces, etc.

The stock for vegetable soup may be water in which vegetables have been previously steamed; or in which beans or grains have been soaked. The term "vegetable broth" refers to homemade stock or any instant vegetable concentrate—powder, packets, or cubes (but no MSG, please!)—diluted in water. Vegetable broth may be substituted for water in all soup recipes (except fruit soup).

Any soup can be thickened in the following manner: Heat a small pan, mix 2 tablespoons oil (or butter) with 2 tablespoons flour (or cornstarch or arrowroot) and stir until brown; then add a small amount of soup liquid and stir until smooth. Add to soup and heat through before serving. For cream soups, milk or cream may be added to the flour mixture.

Soup may be garnished with such diverse items as parsley, watercress, chives; or buttered croutons; or toasted chick peas.

VEGETABLE SOUP
WITH WHEAT BERRY

servings: 6–8
preparation time: at least 2 hours

2 tablespoons butter or oil
1 large onion, diced
3 celery stalks, diced
1 small cabbage, shredded
1 cup wheat berry
8 cups vegetable broth, boiling
3 carrots, sliced
1 turnip, sliced
1 cup chopped parsley
1 clove
1 bay leaf
pinch of nutmeg
salt and pepper to taste

1. In a large pot, sauté onions, celery, and cabbage in butter or oil until golden. Add wheat berry, stirring constantly, until grain is lightly browned.
2. Add broth to pot, cover, and simmer over low heat for ½ hour.
3. Add remaining vegetables and seasoning. Cover pot again and simmer for 1 hour or longer, until vegetables are thoroughly cooked and wheat berry is soft but not mushy. This is a thick soup. It can be made thinner by adding more broth and adjusting seasoning accordingly. Remove bay leaf before serving. Serve hot, topped with buttered croutons.

VARIATION

The recipe above can be revised to make a delicious puréed vegetable soup as follows: Use all the same ingredients but substitute 1 cup green split peas for wheat berry and add peas to broth at the same time as other vegetables. When all vegetables are cooked, remove pot from heat and allow to cool slightly. Then remove bay leaf and spoon all vegetables, together with enough water to blend smoothly, into blender. Purée well and return to pot. Toss in 1 cup of toasted chick peas (optional) and simmer for approximately 15 minutes. Serve hot.

MENU SUGGESTION

Serve with Tomato, Scallions, and Avocado Salad (see page 29).

SPICY INDIAN DAHL SOUP

servings: 8   preparation time: 1 hour

  8 cups water
  1 cup yellow split peas
¼ potato, peeled and grated
  3 potatoes, peeled and sliced thick
oil or clarified butter (ghee)
  1 teaspoon mustard seed
¾ teaspoon cumin
¾ teaspoon coriander
  2 teaspoons turmeric
½ teaspoon cayenne
  1 teaspoon salt

1. Boil split peas and grated potato in water
   until peas are soft. Then purée with a
   beater and add sliced potatoes. Lower heat.
2. While soup is cooking, cover bottom of
   small frying pan with oil or ghee and
   toast mustard seeds until they pop. Mix in
   other spices and stir well.
3. Pour a small amount of soup liquid into
   pan very carefully to avoid splattering.
   Stir well and pour soup-spice mixture
   back into soup.
4. Simmer until potatoes are cooked.
   Serve hot.

MENU SUGGESTIONS

Serve with Chapattis (see page 150) and
Cucumber and Yoghurt (see page 25).

MISO SOUP
WITH CORN AND BEAN SPROUTS

servings: 4   preparation time: 30 minutes

1 tablespoon oil
1 tablespoon cornstarch or arrowroot
1 tablespoon miso (soybean paste)
5 cups boiling water
1 tablespoon tamari sauce
1 teaspoon sugar
1 teaspoon garlic salt
salt and pepper to taste
2 tablespoons Chinese brown sauce or
  molasses
1 pound cooked bean sprouts
1 pound cooked corn

1. In a large pot, heat oil, add cornstarch or
   arrowroot, and stir until smooth.
2. Dilute miso in 1 cup boiling water, add to
   cornstarch, and stir until thickened and
   very smooth.
3. Gradually add remaining water, tamari
   sauce, sugar, and seasoning, stirring
   continuously. If not smooth enough, use
   a beater.
4. Add brown sauce, bean sprouts, and corn.
   Cover and simmer for 15 minutes.
   Serve hot.

VARIATION
To make an excellent sauce for serving over
rice, reduce water to 2 cups instead of 5
and increase cornstarch or arrowroot to
2 tablespoons; follow same procedure as
above.

MENU SUGGESTION
Serve with Egg Rolls (see page 111).

POTATO SOUP

servings: 6   preparation time: 1 hour

  4 large potatoes, peeled and cut in small
    chunks
½ onion, diced
  1 carrot, diced
salt and pepper to taste
  6 cups water
  4 tablespons butter
  4 tablespoons flour
pinch of paprika

1. Slowly boil potatoes, onion, carrot, salt,
   and pepper in water for approximately
   ¾ hour.
2. In a frying pan, melt butter over low heat.
   Add flour and stir continuously until darkly
   browned. Be careful not to burn!
3. Remove pan from heat and gradually add
   one ladleful of soup liquid, stirring until
   smooth; use a beater, if necessary.
4. Add flour mixture and paprika to soup,
   stir well, and bring to a boil. Serve hot.

MENU SUGGESTION

Serve with Artichokes, Egg, and Mayonnaise
(see page 28).

FRESH ASPARAGUS SOUP

servings: 4–6   preparation time: 40 minutes

6 cups water
1½ pounds asparagus, sliced diagonally 1
    inch long
2 egg yolks, beaten
1 tablespoon cornstarch or arrowroot
salt and pepper to taste
pinch of rosemary
2 tablespoons heavy sweet or
    sour cream (optional)

1. In a large pot, bring salted water to a boil,
   add asparagus, and cook over low heat
   until tender yet still crisp. Remove from
   water and place on a plate.
2. Combine egg yolks and cornstarch or
   arrowroot and pour slowly into water.
   Stir continuously, over low heat, until liquid
   is smooth and creamy. Add seasoning
   and asparagus. Simmer until asparagus is
   well cooked.
3. If desired, stir in two tablespoons heavy
   sweet or sour cream just before serving.
   Serve hot.

MENU SUGGESTION

Serve with Viennese Cheese Dumplings
(see page 68).

ALL-GREEN-VEGETABLE SOUP

servings: 4   preparation time: 45 minutes

  2 tablespoons oil or butter
  1 onion, sliced
  1 garlic clove, minced
  2 celery stalks and leaves, chopped
  4 cups vegetable broth
½ pound each string beans and peas
  1 bunch parsley, chopped fine
  1 bay leaf
  2 sprigs each rosemary and thyme
pinch of nutmeg
salt and pepper to taste

1. Sauté onion and garlic in oil or butter
   until golden. Add celery and stir for a few
   minutes. Drain off any excess oil.
2. Meanwhile, snap beans in half and shell
   peas.
3. In a large pot, bring broth to a boil and
   add all ingredients. Bring to a boil again;
   cover and simmer until beans and peas
   are tender.
4. Remove bay leaf and stalks of herbs.
   Adjust seasoning and serve hot.

SWEET CREAM OF CARROT SOUP

servings: 4   preparation time: 50 minutes

1 pound carrots, chopped
4 cups water or vegetable broth
salt and pepper to taste
1 teaspoon honey
1 egg yolk
4 tablespoons light sweet cream
1 tablespoon butter

1. Bring carrots and water or broth to a boil.
   Cover pot, lower heat, and simmer for
   approximately ½ hour.
2. When carrots are tender, remove them
   from water and purée either in a food mill
   or blender. Return carrots to water and
   bring to a boil.
3. Add seasoning and honey.
4. Beat egg yolk and cream together in
   a small bowl.
5. Remove soup from heat and slowly stir
   in egg mixture and butter. Heat through
   but do not boil. Serve hot or cold.

LENTIL AND SWEET POTATO SOUP

servings: 4   preparation time: 1 hour

  1 cup lentils
  4 cups water
  1 large sweet potato, peeled and
     sliced ½ inch thick
¼ teaspoon sugar
salt and pepper to taste

1. Wash lentils well and boil in salted water
   until soft.
2. Remove lentils from water and mash
   through a strainer. Discard skins.
3. Return mashed lentils to cooking water.
4. Add sweet potato slices, sugar and
   seasoning. Boil until potatoes are cooked.
   Serve hot.

MUSHROOM, BEAN, AND BARLEY SOUP

servings: 6   preparation time: 2 hours

1 large onion, diced
1 garlic clove, minced
2 tablespoons butter or oil
½ pound mushrooms, sliced
6 cups vegetable broth, boiling
½ cup dried lima beans, soaked for
   several hours
1 cup barley
1 bunch parsley, chopped fine
pinch each of nutmeg, thyme, and ginger
1 clove
salt and pepper to taste

1. In a large pot, sauté onion and garlic in
   butter or oil until golden.
2. Add mushrooms, lower heat, and cook
   covered for 10 minutes
3. Add broth and remaining ingredients.
   Cover and simmer for 1½ hours. Serve hot.

NOTE

A dark broth adds richness to this soup.
If a thinner soup is desired, add more broth.

VARIATION

To turn this into a cream soup, make
Basic Cream Sauce (see page 167) using
1 tablespoon butter, 1 tablespoon flour, and
1 cup milk. Mix with a little broth, stir into
soup, and heat through just before serving.

MENU SUGGESTION

Serve with French Green Beans and
Sunflower Seeds (see page 104).

COLD QUICK "REAL" BORSCHT

servings: 4   preparation time: 10 minutes

1 large jar pickled beets, chilled
1 large jar plain beets, chilled
1 large can vegetable juice, chilled
3 tablespoons chopped fresh dill
sour cream

1. Pour beets and beet liquid into blender
   and chop.
2. Pour in juice and blend well.
3. Serve chilled, topped with dill and
   sour cream.

QUICK COLD GAZPACHO

servings: 4   preparation time: 15 minutes
(not including chilling)

1 green pepper, cut in quarters
4 tomatoes, cut in quarters
½ small cucumber, cut in half
1 small onion, cut in half
6 garlic cloves, cut in half
1 cup olive oil
¼ cup vinegar
3 hard rolls or 4 pieces stale bread,
    soaked in water
salt to taste

1. Purée first five ingredients in a blender
   or food mill. Add oil and vinegar and
   continue to blend.
2. Break off small pieces of rolls or bread,
   squeeze out a little water, and add to
   blender. Continue blending until all bread
   is used up. Add salt.
3. Strain. If soup tastes too strong, add cold
   water. Chill and serve with garnishes.

GARNISHES
1 small onion, diced fine
½ small cucumber, diced fine
1 green pepper, diced fine
croutons

CREAM OF WATERCRESS SOUP

servings: 6   preparation time: 50 minutes

    4 tablespoons butter
    1 garlic clove, minced
    1 onion or 2 leeks, chopped
    6 potatoes, peeled and sliced thin
    salt and pepper to taste
    1 cup water
    1 bunch watercress
2½ cups water
1½ cups milk
    2 egg yolks
  ½ cup light sweet cream

1. In a large pot, sauté garlic and onion or
   leeks in butter until golden.
2. Add potatoes, seasoning, and one cup of
   water. Cover and boil; then reduce heat and
   cook until potatoes are almost tender,
   approximately 15 minutes.
3. Reserve half the watercress leaves. Add
   remaining leaves and stems, milk and
   water. Simmer for 15 minutes; then remove
   and purée in food mill or blender. Return
   to pot.
4. Blend egg yolks and cream together.
   Gradually add to soup, stirring
   continuously, until soup is slightly
   thickened. Heat through but do not boil.
5. Spoon into bowls and top with reserved
   watercress leaves. Serve hot or chilled.

COLD FRESH CHERRY SOUP

servings: 4   preparation time: 25 minutes
(not including chilling)

1½ pounds sour cherries, stems removed
   3 eggs, separated
   4 tablespoons sugar
   4 cups water
   1 lemon rind, sliced

1. Boil cherries for 15 minutes.
2. Meanwhile, beat egg yolks with sugar
   until pale yellow and creamy. Then pour
   slowly into soup, stirring constantly.
3. Whip egg whites until stiff and fold in
   carefully.
4. Add lemon rind. Taste and add more sugar
   if necessary.
5. Chill and remove rind before serving.

VARIATION

For a richer soup, just before serving add
6 tablespoons sour cream and beat well. For
a thinner soup, increase amount of water.
Plums or peaches may be substituted for
cherries.

chapter 3
EGGS, CHEESE, AND PASTA

Eggs and cheese have an important function in a vegetarian diet, for they provide necessary protein. Besides their obvious food value, they are among the most versatile and attractive of ingredients. Cheese can appear gracefully at any point of the meal, as appetizer, salad, main course, or dessert.

Try to use fresh, untreated eggs from organically fed hens. The difference in taste may astound you! *Important*: Refrigerate eggs immediately and cook them slowly to retain their flavor.

Try to purchase noodles, macaroni and spaghetti made from stone-ground whole-grain flours. Whole wheat noodles add a unique texture and flavor to any pasta dish.

Most kinds of pasta may be interchanged in any of the following recipes.

EGGS A LA RUSSE

servings: 4   preparation time: 5 minutes

4 hard-cooked eggs, chilled and sliced
    in half lengthwise
1 small jar red caviar
2 lemons, sliced thin

DRESSING
6 tablespoons mayonnaise
2 tablespoons chili sauce or 2 tablespoons
    ketchup mixed with 1 teaspoon relish
1 teaspoon chopped chives

1. Blend all dressing ingredients well.
2. On a bed of lettuce, place 2 egg halves;
    spoon dressing over them. Top with caviar.
3. Serve chilled with lemon slices as an
    appetizer or salad.

PLAIN AND FILLED OMELETTES

servings: 2
preparation time: varies with omelette

4 eggs
2 tablespoons butter
1 tablespoon light sweet cream (optional)
dash of vanilla
salt and pepper to taste

1. Beat eggs, cream (if used),and seasoning until eggs are pale yellow and foamy.
2. Heat an omelette pan* and melt butter over low heat.
3. Pour eggs in pan, moving pan back and forth with one hand, stirring eggs with a fork in a circular motion with the other hand. Continue until bottom of eggs are set and tops are moist. If a filling is used (see below), place it on one half of the omelette—the side nearest you. Tilt the pan back slightly and roll the omelette with a fork or spatula away from you. When rolled, turn omelette quickly onto a warmed plate.

FILLINGS

Omelettes can be made with a variety of fillings; here are a few samples.

Cheddar or Swiss cheese: Use ½ cup, grated.

Mushrooms: Use 5 or 6, sliced and sautéed in butter, with or without Cream Sauce (see page 167).

Mushrooms and onions: Prepare as above with 1 small onion.

Spinach: Use 1 cup, chopped; steam in butter or mix with a little sour cream and garlic salt.

Asparagus: Use 3 or 4 stalks, steam in butter (or cooked leftovers) with Cream Sauce (see page 167).

Cucumber: Use 1 medium. Scoop out seeds; stew in Cream Sauce (see page 167).

NOTE

When using Cream Sauce, blend in just enough to make vegetables creamy and serve remainder over cooked omelette.

VARIATION

Roll omelette in grated Parmesan cheese. Place on buttered toast and sprinkle with more cheese. Put on a cookie sheet and place in hot (400°) oven for approximately two minutes, or until top is browned. Serve plain or with tomato sauce.

MENU SUGGESTION

Serve with Cold Fresh Cherry Soup (see page 55).

*Omelettes should be made in an omelette pan or a frying pan with rounded sides that is reserved for cooking omelettes only. The pan should never be washed, just wiped with a cloth or paper towel. If eggs begin to stick, "season" the pan as follows: Place on very high heat and sprinkle liberally with coarse salt; then remove from heat and, while it's still hot, wipe briskly with a clean cloth.

SHIRRED EGGS

serving: 1   preparation time: 15 minutes

1 teaspoon butter
2 eggs
1 slice tomato
1 slice Swiss or Cheddar cheese
1 teaspoon grated Parmesan cheese or
    1 teaspoon heavy sweet cream
salt to taste

1. Preheat oven to 375°
2. Spoon butter into a small casserole and place in oven until butter is melted.
3. Break eggs into a bowl, remove casserole from oven, and slide eggs carefully into casserole.
4. Place tomato, cheese, and grated cheese or cream on top and put back into oven.
5. Bake until whites have set. Season and serve hot.

VARIATION

Add a bit of cooked spinach or asparagus to tomato and cheese for a whole meal in one dish.

MENU SUGGESTION

Serve with Stuffed Tomatoes (see page 24).

BAKED EGGS A LA FLAMENCO

servings: 4   preparation time: 40 minutes

2 potatoes, diced small
2 tablespoons olive oil
1 cup peas, cooked
4 pimientos, diced
½ pound asparagus, cooked (optional)
2 cups homemade or canned tomato sauce
8 eggs
salt to taste

1. Fry potatoes as for Miguel's Authentic
   Spanish Omelette (see page 63).
2. Preheat oven to 325°.
3. Grease four small casseroles and line
   with fried potatoes. Add remaining
   vegetables in separate layers and pour
   tomato sauce over everything.
4. For each casserole break two eggs into
   a bowl and slide carefully on top.
5. Bake for 15–20 minutes, until whites have
   set. Salt after baking and serve straight
   from the oven.

MENU SUGGESTION

Serve with Mediterranean Salad
(see page 22).

MIGUEL'S AUTHENTIC SPANISH OMELETTE

serving: 1   preparation time: 30 minutes

  1 small potato, diced fine and salted
  2 tablespoons oil (the Spanish always use
     olive oil)
½ small onion, diced fine
  2 eggs, separated
salt and pepper to taste

1. In a small frying pan, heat oil well and
   fry potato over medium heat until
   partially soft and golden, approximately
   10 minutes. Drain and set aside.
2. In the same oil, fry onion until golden.
   Drain and set aside.
3. In a bowl, beat egg whites until foamy.
   Separately, beat yolks until pale yellow;
   combine whites and yolks.
4. Add potato, onion, and seasoning.
   Mix well.
5. Add a bit more oil to the same pan and
   heat over high heat. Pour mixture into pan
   and lower to medium heat. Tilt pan
   back and forth to distribute mixture evenly,
   and cook slowly until eggs are almost
   set and not runny.
6. Place a flat plate or pan cover over pan
   and flip omelette onto it. Then slide
   omelette back into pan and cook for a few
   minutes longer until slightly browned.
7. Remove from pan and serve hot or cold.

NOTE

A large omelette for several people can be
made by increasing the above ingredients
proportionately and cooking in a large
frying pan; then cut into individual slices.

MENU SUGGESTION

Serve with Quick Cold Gazpacho
(see page 51).

BUTTERLESS SCRAMBLED EGGS

servings: 2   preparation time: 8–10 minutes

4 tablespoons milk
3 eggs
salt and pepper to taste

1. In a frying pan, heat milk to the boiling
   point; then lower heat.
2. Beat eggs with salt and pepper and add
   to milk. Stir, cover, and let cook for
   approximately 3 minutes. Serve on
   warmed plates.

BAKED CHEESE PANCAKES

yield: 8–10 pancakes
preparation time: 30 minutes

  1 pound farmer cheese
½ pound cream cheese
½ cup sugar
  2 eggs
  1 teaspoon vanilla
  1 cup wheat germ or Grain Cereal
      (see page 184)

1. Preheat oven to 375°.
2. Mix cheeses with sugar, eggs, and vanilla
   until well blended.
3. Form mixture into small balls and flatten
   into ½-inch-thick pancakes.
4. Roll cakes in wheat germ or Grain Cereal
   and place on a greased cookie sheet.
5. Bake for 20 minutes. Serve hot—plain or
   with fresh crushed strawberries.

NOTE

Uncooked pancakes may be stored in
refrigerator for four or five days and then
baked as needed.

MENU SUGGESTION

Serve as a dessert or as a main dish for
lunch or supper with Cold Quick "Real"
Borscht (see page 50) or Cold Fresh
Cherry Soup (see page 55).

CHEESE BLINTZES

yield: 10–12 blintzes
preparation time: 1 hour

BATTER:
   3 eggs, beaten lightly
   1 cup flour
1½ cups milk
salt to taste

FILLING:
1 pound cottage cheese
1 pound farmer cheese
2 egg yolks, beaten
1 tablespoon butter
1 tablespoon lemon juice
1 tablespoon lemon rind, grated
5 tablespoons sugar

1. Blend batter ingredients in a mixing bowl
   and set aside.
2. Lightly grease a small frying pan and
   warm over medium heat.
3. Pour in 1 ladleful of batter and tilt pan
   until batter covers bottom entirely. Allow
   a thin layer to adhere to bottom and
   quickly pour excess back into bowl.
   Cook "leaf" on one side only until it
   blisters, then flip onto plate, fried side up.
   Repeat process until all "leaves" are
   cooked. Keep pan lightly greased
   throughout.
4. Mix all filling ingredients in a bowl and
   put about 1 tablespoon of filling in center
   of each leaf. Fold all sides over each

other and form into envelope shape.
5. Before serving, fry on both sides or bake
   in a medium oven until golden brown.
   Serve with sour cream, berry preserves, or
   fresh strawberries.

NOTE

Blintzes can be stored in freezer before
frying. Fry without defrosting when ready.

VARIATION

A batter can be made with 1 egg by
combining the following ingredients.

BATTER:
   1 egg
   1 cup milk
1½ cups flour
   4 tablespoons butter
   1 cup water
salt to taste

FILLING:
Same as above
Follow directions above.

MENU SUGGESTION

This can be served for dessert, or as a
main course for lunch or supper with
Cold Quick "Real" Borscht (see page 50), or
Cold Fresh Cherry Soup (see page 55).

VIENNESE CHEESE DUMPLINGS (TOPFENKNODEL)

yield: 8 dumplings
preparation time: 45 minutes

½ pound farmer cheese, at room temperature
4 tablespoons butter
1 egg
1 cup flour
1 tablespoon sugar
salt to taste

1. Mix all ingredients well and allow to stand for ½ hour.
2. Boil water and salt in a large pot. Form batter into balls and drop into water. Boil slowly for 10 minutes.
3. Carefully remove dumplings from water and place in a warm greased bowl or casserole. Sprinkle with cinnamon and sugar; or grated cheese; or nuts and sugar.

ITALIAN CHEESE AND POTATO PIE

servings: 4   preparation time: 1 hour

  4 potatoes, peeled and cut in small chunks
½ cup light sweet cream
  3 tablespoons butter
  1 egg, separated
½ cup chopped parsley
salt and pepper to taste
½ cup seasoned bread crumbs
½ pound Mozzarella cheese
½ cup grated Parmesan cheese

1. Preheat oven to 375°.
2. Boil potatoes, drain, and mash well with
   cream and butter.
3. Beat egg yolk and mix with potatoes.
4. Whip egg white stiff with a pinch of salt
   and fold into potatoes with seasoning
   and parsley.
5. Grease a pie plate and sprinkle bottom
   liberally with bread crumbs. Then place
   potato mixture and sliced Mozzarella in
   alternate layers, starting with potatoes and
   finishing with cheese.
6. Sprinkle top with grated Parmesan
   cheese and dot with butter.
7. Bake for approximately 45 minutes until
   top is golden brown. Serve hot.

MENU SUGGESTION

Serve with Fried Green Peppers
(see page 85).

PASTA AND BEANS

servings: 4   preparation time: 40 minutes
                    (not including soaking)

2 tablespoons each of olive oil and
    vegetable oil
1 onion, chopped
3 garlic cloves, minced
1 cup dried beans (such as navy, white, or
    chick peas), soaked 6 hours; or 1½ cups
    cooked beans
1 pound any small-size macaroni
salt and pepper to taste
½ eggplant or yellow squash, cooked and
    chopped (optional)
2 tomatoes, seeded and chopped
2 cups vegetable broth
1 teaspoon dried hot red pepper

1. Sauté onion and garlic in oil until brown.
2. If using dried beans, combine them with
   onion and garlic, cover with water, and
   cook until tender. If using cooked beans,
   use a small amount of liquid, combine with
   onions and garlic, and cook briefly over
   low heat.
3. Cook macaroni until parboiled. Drain.
4. Place macaroni, bean mixture and other
   vegetables in a large pot. Add vegetable
   broth and seasoning and cook over medium
   heat for about 10 minutes, or until
   macaroni is al dente. Serve hot.

VARIATIONS

For a stronger tomato flavor, add
1 tablespoon tomato paste to vegetables
before final step. If you increase the amount
of vegetable broth and serve in bowls,
this dish becomes a soup.

MENU SUGGESTION

Serve with Grapefruit and Avocado Salad
(see page 27).

NOODLE PUDDING 1

servings: 4   preparation time: 1 hour

½ pound broad noodles
3 tablespoons butter
3 eggs, separated
¾ cup sugar or ½ cup honey
1 teaspoon cinnamon
2 apples, sliced and sprinkled with
   lemon juice
½ cup currants or raisins
½ cup chopped walnuts or toasted almonds
salt to taste

1. Preheat oven to 350°.
2. Boil noodles in salted water for 15–20
   minutes, until cooked yet firm.
3. Drain and run under cold water.
4. In a large frying pan, melt butter and
   toss noodles gently (try not to break them)
   until all butter is evenly distributed and
   absorbed.
5. Meanwhile, beat egg yolks and combine
   with other ingredients.
6. Remove noodles from heat and toss well
   with egg mixture.
7. Whip egg whites stiff and slowly fold in.
8. Turn into a greased casserole and bake
   for ½ hour. Serve hot or cold.

NOODLE PUDDING 2

servings: 4   preparation time: 1 hour

½ pound broad noodles
  6 tablespoons butter, at room temperature
  3 eggs, separated
½ pound farmer cheese
½ cup sour cream
salt, pepper and paprika to taste

1. Preheat oven to 350°.
2. Prepare noodles as in Noodle Pudding 1
   recipe, using 3 tablespoons butter.
3. Combine beaten egg yolks, cheese,
   sour cream, seasonings, and remaining
   butter. Add to noodles and toss well.
4. Whip egg whites stiff and fold in.
5. Turn into a greased casserole and bake
   for ½ hour. Serve hot.

VARIATION

Buttered bread crumbs sprinkled on bottom
of casserole before adding noodles and
baking make this dish particularly rich and
delicious.

MENU SUGGESTION

Serve with Cream of Watercress Soup
(see page 54).

NOODLES WITH CABBAGE

servings: 4–6   preparation time: 30 minutes

1 pound broad noodles
1 large onion, diced
6 tablespoons butter
1 small cabbage, shredded
salt and pepper to taste
2 tablespoons poppy seeds
2 tablespoons sour cream
1 tablespoon grated Parmesan cheese
  (optional)

1. Cook noodles in boiling salted water.
   Drain and set aside.
2. Sauté onion in 4 tablespoons butter
   until golden.
3. Add cabbage and cook over low heat,
   stirring occasionally, until tender.
4. Add noodles and mix well with remaining
   butter.
5. Mix in seasoning, poppy seeds, sour cream,
   and cheese. Cover and heat through.
   Serve hot.

MENU SUGGESTION

Serve with All-Green-Vegetable Soup
(see page 45).

SPAGHETTI AL PESTO

servings: 4–6   preparation time: 15 minutes
                    (not including chilling)

  1 pound spinach
½ pound fresh basil
  1 cup olive oil (best quality)
  3 garlic cloves
¼ cup grated Romano cheese
¼ cup pine nuts
  2 pounds spaghetti

1. Place all ingredients, except spaghetti,
   in blender and purée thoroughly.
2. Chill for at least 1 hour.
3. When ready to serve, cook spaghetti, add a
   teaspoon of butter per serving, and pour
   sauce over spaghetti; toss well and serve
   immediately.

VARIATION

Parsley and watercress may be substituted
for spinach—but *fresh* basil is essential!

NOTE

Extra sauce may be stored in the refrigerator
for up to 2 weeks.

chapter 4 VEGETABLES

Vegetables are the staple of the vegetarian diet. They provide a wealth of vitamins and minerals and can be prepared in a vast number of ways. Ideally, we should raise our own vegetables. Since this is impractical for many, the next best thing is to buy organically grown, preferably locally grown, vegetables. Don't be put off by some that may have a limp, shriveled appearance. Remember, these vegetables are free of preservatives, sprays and coloring. This may cause them to look "tired," but it's only because some of the water has evaporated. Buy them! They *do* taste better.

Most of the recipes that follow begin with fresh, well-scrubbed and unpeeled vegetables. The two cooking methods I use most often to prepare simple vegetables quickly and to best conserve their natural goodness are:

STEAMING, using either a pressure cooker or vegetable steamer (see page 9). If you are using the steamer, put no more than ½ inch salted water or vegetable broth in a heavy pot with a lid; bring to a boil; place vegetables in steamer; lower heat and cover tightly. Steam until vegetable is tender but not mushy—what the Italians call "al dente," which, freely translated, means that you need teeth to eat it. Cooking time will vary with the vegetable (green beans usually take 15 minutes; beets, 30 minutes).

QUICK-SAUTÉEING, which works best when vegetables are finely sliced or cut in strips. Heat a small amount of oil (1 tablespoon is usually enough) in a pan, add vegetables and cook for approximately 5 minutes over high heat. Lower heat to medium, cook another 10 minutes, stirring continuously; then add a little water, cover and simmer until tender. The amount of time and water will depend on the type and size of the vegetables being cooked. The addition of tamari sauce at the last minute enhances the taste of many quick-sautéed vegetables.

Avoid boiling vegetables except in soups, stews, and sauces. A good rule is to cook with as little water and in as short a time as possible.

In addition to the recipes in this chapter, you will find other vegetables and ways of preparing them on pages 11—15.

SAVOY CABBAGE AND POTATOES

servings: 4   preparation time: 45 minutes

1 Savoy cabbage, cut in small chunks
4 cups water
4 potatoes, peeled and diced fine
salt to taste
2 tablespoons oil
2 tablespoons flour
1 garlic clove, minced
pinch of pepper

1. Boil cabbage in salted water for approximately 10 minutes.
2. Add potatoes and boil vegetables together until potatoes are cooked. Drain but reserve cooking water.
3. In a small frying pan, heat oil, add flour, and stir continuously until well browned. Add some cooking water and stir until smooth.
4. Combine cabbage, potatoes, browned flour, and at least 2 cups of cooking water. Add garlic and seasoning and mash all ingredients thoroughly. Mixture should be moist, add more water if necessary.
5. Heat through and serve hot.

MENU SUGGESTION

Serve with Honeyed Carrots (see page 101).

JAPANESE TEMPURA

servings: 4–6   preparation time: 30 minutes

BATTER:
 1 cup flour
 2 eggs, beaten
½ cup water, very cold
¼ cup tamari sauce
½ teaspoon salt

VEGETABLES (use no more than four
    varieties at one meal):
broccoli, broken into small flowerlets
carrots, sliced into ½-inch-wide, 1-inch-long
    strips
cauliflower, broken into small flowerlets
eggplant, sliced horizontally, ½ inch wide
green pepper, sliced in ½-inch-wide strips
mushroom caps, whole
onions, sliced in ½-inch-wide rings
zucchini, sliced horizontally, ½ inch wide

peanut oil
tamari sauce

1. Prepare batter by blending all ingredients
   thoroughly.

2. Choose vegetables. Dip into batter and
   coat well.
3. Pour at least three inches of oil in a large
   frying pan and fry vegetables, one variety
   at a time, until golden brown. (*Note:* Oil
   must be *very* hot—test by dropping in a bit
   of batter. When batter bubbles on contact,
   oil is ready.) Cooking time will vary;
   carrots, eggplant, and mushrooms take
   longest.
4. Drain on paper towel and serve as quickly
   as possible with tamari sauce on the side.

NOTE

Leftover batter can be dropped by spoonfuls
into oil, fried, and eaten like popovers,
or stored in refrigerator for future use.

MENU SUGGESTION

Serve with plain rice and Cucumber and
Yoghurt Salad (see page 25).

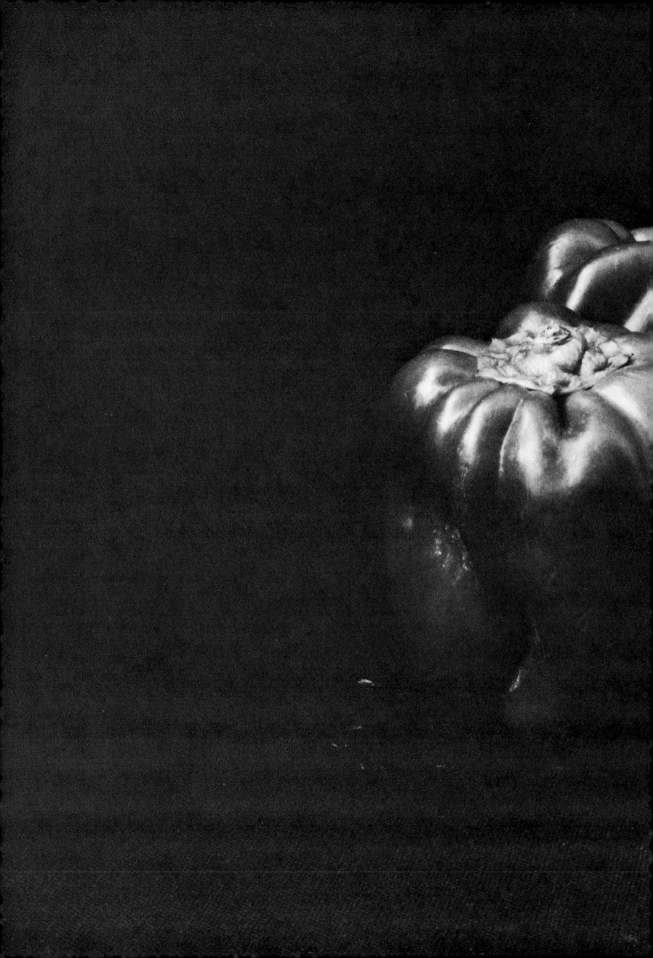

POTATO PANCAKES (LATKES)

yield: about 20 pancakes
preparation time: 30 minutes

1 large onion, sliced thin
oil
6 large potatoes, peeled and grated
4 heaping tablespoons pancake flour
2 eggs, slightly beaten
1 onion, grated
salt and pepper to taste

1. Fry onion slices lightly in hot deep oil.
2. Mix remaining ingredients well.
3. For each pancake spoon 1 heaping
   tablespoon of batter into oil, flattening
   pancake with a spoon immediately.
4. Fry for approximately 5 minutes on each
   side, or until brown and crispy.
5. Drain on paper towel and serve hot.

FRIED GREEN PEPPERS

servings: 4–6   preparation time: 15 minutes

  6 large or 12 small green peppers
salt to taste
  4 garlic cloves, whole
½ cup olive oil

1. Remove stem and seeds from peppers in the following manner. Push in stem until it feels loose. Then quickly pull out stem with seeds. Cut large peppers in quarters, small peppers in halves, lengthwise. Season.
2. In a large frying pan, brown garlic in hot oil.
3. Over medium heat, fry peppers until tender and well browned.
4. Drain on paper towel and serve immediately.

NOTE

For a decorative splash, after step 3 add pimientos or cooked sweet red peppers and heat through.

VEGETARIAN SHISHKEBAB

servings: 4–6   preparation time: 3 hours

MARINADE:
½ cup tamari sauce
¼ cup water
 1 tablespoon curry powder
 1 teaspoon ginger
 1 bay leaf
 1 onion, sliced thin
 2 garlic cloves, minced
Pinch each of salt and pepper

VEGETABLES:
 5 large tomatoes, cubed; or
   20 cherry tomatoes
 4 green peppers, seeds removed and cubed
 2 large onions, cut in small chunks; or
   12 whole small white onions
½ pound mushrooms, caps only

1. Blend all marinade ingredients well.
2. Place vegetables in a deep bowl and cover
   with marinade. If more liquid is required,
   increase tamari sauce and water
   proportionately.
3. Cover bowl and leave in a cool place—
   do not refrigerate—for at least 2 hours.
4. Remove vegetables from marinade and
   place alternately on skewers. Broil or
   barbecue, basting with marinade, until
   vegetables are tender and well browned.
   Serve hot over rice.

ARABIAN-STYLE VEGETABLES

servings: 4   preparation time: 30 minutes

¼ cup peanut oil
 1 large onion, sliced thin
 2 garlic cloves, minced
 1 tomato, peeled and diced
 1 small cauliflower, broken into flowerlets
½ pound string beans, snapped in half
 2 potatoes, peeled and diced small
salt and pepper to taste

1. Heat oil in a deep frying pan, and
   sauté onions and garlic until golden.
2. Add tomato and sauté until tender.
3. Add remaining vegetables, seasoning, and
   a little water.
4. Cover and simmer until vegetables are
   tender. If mixture begins to dry out,
   add more water. Serve hot.

CHILLED ZUCCHINI

servings: 4   preparation time: 20 minutes
(not including chilling)

4 small zucchini, sliced diagonally,
   ¼ inch thick
1 tablespoon chopped fresh mint or
   1 tablespoon dried mint
2 tablespoons chopped fresh dill or
   1 tablespoon dill weed
⅓ cup olive oil

1. Combine zucchini with herbs and sauté
   in oil until tender and golden.
2. Allow to cool, chill, and serve with lots
   of plain yoghurt.

CORN FRITTERS

servings: 4   preparation time: 20 minutes

  2 eggs, separated
salt and pepper to taste
  2 cups cooked corn
  3 tablespoons flour or meal or 2 tablespoons
     flour and 1 tablespoon wheat germ
  3 tablespoons milk or 3½ tablespoons
     heavy sweet cream
½ teaspoon vanilla
½ cup peanut or vegetable oil

1. Beat egg yolks with a pinch of salt and
   combine with corn, flour or meal, milk,
   pepper, and vanilla.
2. Whip egg whites with a pinch of salt until
   stiff and fold into corn mixture.
3. In a deep frying pan, heat oil until very
   hot. Drop mixture by tablespoonfuls and
   fry on both sides over high heat until
   crisp. Drain on paper towel. Serve
   immediately topped with sugar or honey.

TOP-OF-THE-STOVE POTATO PUDDING

servings: 4   preparation time: 40 minutes

  1 pound potatoes, peeled and grated
  1 onion, grated
  2 eggs, beaten
salt and pepper to taste
  2 tablespoons flour or meal
¼ cup oil
  1 onion, sliced thin
½ cup chopped parsley

1. Mix potatoes and grated onion together.
2. Add eggs, seasoning, and flour or meal. Mixture should pour easily but not be too liquid—add more flour if necessary.
3. In a large deep frying pan, heat oil over high heat and brown sliced onion and parsley.
4. Pour in potato mixture, reduce to medium heat, and cook for approximately 15 minutes, or until top is not runny, and bottom is crisply browned.
5. Take pan to the sink and cover with a large plate. Flip pan over and then slide pudding back into pan, cooked side up. Return to heat and continue cooking until bottom is browned and potatoes are thoroughly cooked.
6. Serve hot with or without Brown Sauce (see page 168).

MENU SUGGESTION

Serve with Oriental Spinach (see page 97).

JERUSALEM ARTICHOKES

servings: 4   preparation time: 10 minutes

  4 tablespoons butter
¼ cup water
  1 pound Jerusalem artichokes, sliced
    ¼ inch thick
salt and pepper to taste

1. Melt butter and add water, artichokes, and seasoning.
2. Cover tightly and simmer until tender yet crisp.
3. Serve with Cheese Sauce (see page 167).

SOUR CREAM MUSHROOMS

servings: 4   preparation time: 10 minutes

  1 pound mushrooms
  1 small onion, diced
  3 tablespoons butter
salt and pepper to taste
  2 tablespoons white cooking wine
  2 tablespoons cooking sherry
¾ cup sour cream
  1 tablespoon minced chives
  3 tablespoons diced cucumber

1. Leave small mushrooms whole; cut large
   ones in half.
2. Sauté mushrooms and onion in butter for
   approximately 5 minutes.
3. Add seasoning and wines and cook over
   low heat for 1 minute longer.
4. Add sour cream, chives, and cucumbers.
   Mix thoroughly and heat. Serve hot.

MENU SUGGESTION

Serve with buttered noodles or Noodles with
Cabbage (see page 76).

BRUSSELS SPROUTS, WATER CHESTNUTS, AND MUSHROOMS

servings: 4   preparation time: 30 minutes

 1 pound Brussels sprouts
 2 tablespoons butter
½ pound mushrooms, sliced
 1 can (6 ounces) water chestnuts, drained
 1 teaspoon thyme
½ teaspoon ginger
½ cup pine nuts (optional)
salt and pepper to taste

1. Steam sprouts until tender.
2. In a separate pan, sauté mushrooms, chestnuts, and pine nuts in butter. Add seasoning, cover, and cook until mushrooms are tender.
3. Dish sprouts onto plate and carefully place mushroom mixture on top. Serve hot.

MUSHROOM CAPS BAKED IN CHEDDAR CHEESE SAUCE

servings: 4   preparation time: 30 minutes

1 garlic clove, diced
3 tablespoons butter
1 pound mushrooms, caps only
salt and pepper to taste
dash of Worcestershire sauce
Cheese Sauce (see page 167), double recipe
pinch of cayenne

1. Preheat oven to 350°.
2. Sauté garlic lightly in butter until soft;
   then discard garlic.
3. Add mushroom caps and seasoning to
   butter, cook over low heat, covered,
   until tender.
4. Prepare a double recipe of Cheese Sauce,
   using Cheddar cheese and adding cayenne.
5. Transfer mushroom caps to a greased
   casserole, cover with sauce, and place
   in oven for a few minutes until top is
   lightly browned and bubbly. Serve hot.

ORIENTAL SPINACH

servings: 4   preparation time: 15 minutes

3 tablespoons peanut oil
2 garlic cloves, minced
1 pound spinach, torn
1 teaspoon sugar
2 teaspoons salt

1. In a large deep frying pan brown garlic
   in hot oil.
2. Add spinach and toss well so that oil is
   evenly distributed.
3. Add sugar and salt, toss again, and cook
   over medium heat. Stir frequently and
   cook until spinach is tender but not soggy,
   approximately five minutes. Serve
   immediately.

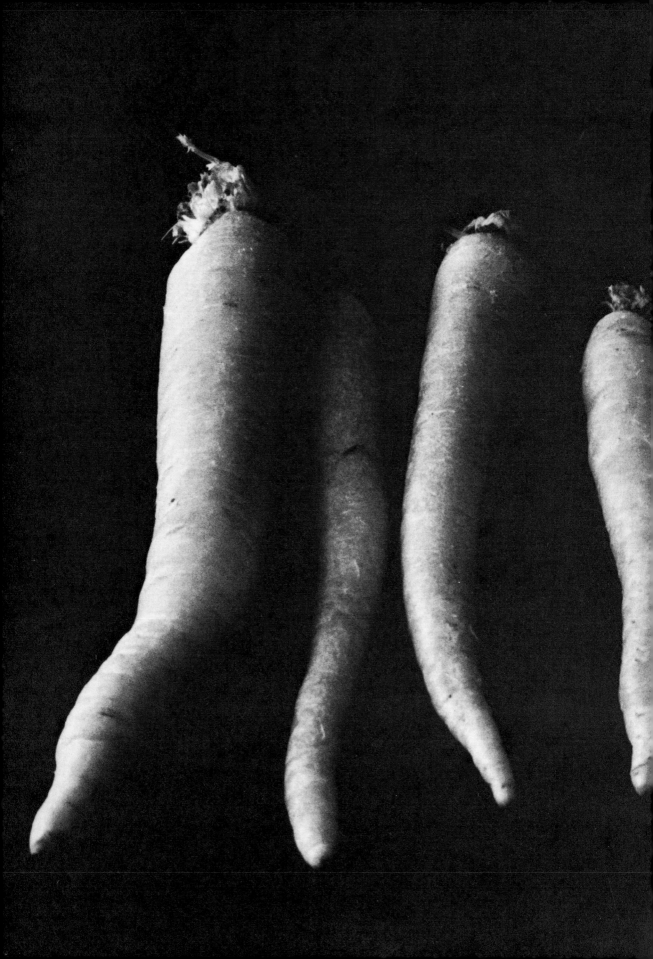

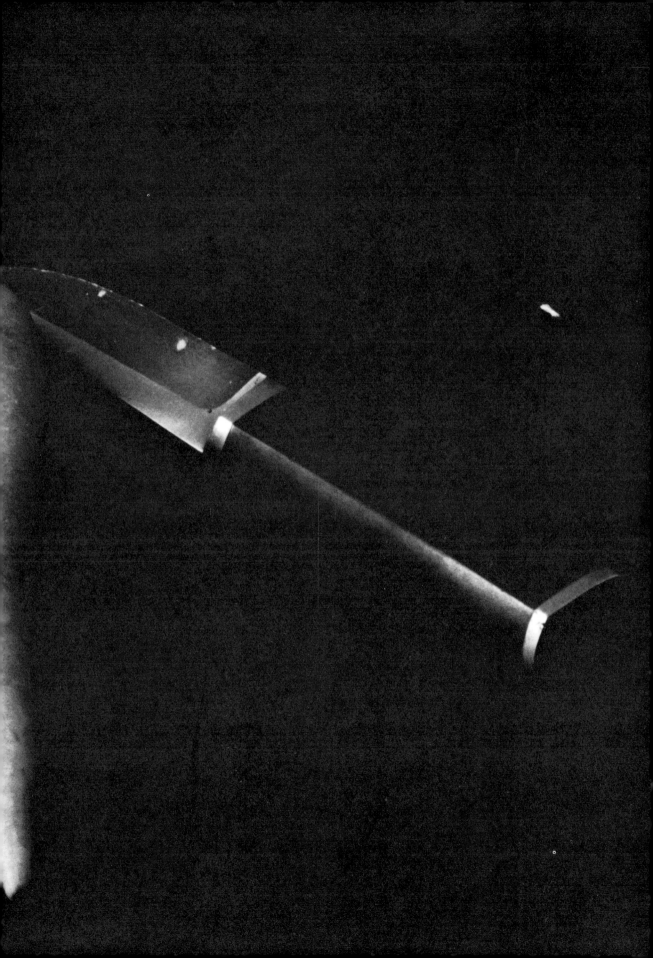

SPINACH DUMPLINGS

servings: 4
preparation time: at least 2¼ hours

1 pound spinach, chopped
2 eggs, beaten
pinch each of oregano and sage
salt to taste
flour
2 cups croutons, browned in butter
¼ cup oil

1. Steam spinach until tender and drain well.
2. Combine spinach with remaining ingredients, using just enough flour to give mixture a soft, biscuit-like texture.
3. Cover mixture and chill for at least 2 hours.
4. When ready to serve, wet hands and form mixture into small balls. Boil in salted water for 10–15 minutes.
5. Serve hot in Tomato Sauce (see page 165) or bake briefly in oven.

VARIATION

Sauté spinach dumplings in mixture of 3 tablespoons oil and 1 tablespoon minced garlic clove until browned. Drain and serve.

MENU SUGGESTION

Serve with Sweet Cream of Carrot Soup (see page 46).

HONEYED CARROTS

servings: 4   preparation time: 20 minutes

4 carrots
2 tablespoons butter
2 tablespoons honey

1. Slice carrots horizontally about ¼ inch
   thick. Then cut pieces into thirds so that
   carrots resemble thin matchsticks.
2. In a frying pan, melt butter, add carrots,
   and cover. Sauté approximately 5 minutes.
3. Add honey, stir well, cover again, and
   sauté over low heat until tender—
   approximately 10 minutes.

SWEET AND SOUR CABBAGE

servings: 4   preparation time: 20 minutes

4 tablespoons butter
1 small cabbage, shredded
1 egg
2 tablespoons sugar
1 cup sour cream
1 teaspoon prepared or freshly grated
  horseradish
salt and pepper to taste
2 tablespoons lemon juice

1. In a large frying pan, melt butter.
2. Add cabbage and cook over low heat,
   stirring occasionally until tender yet slightly
   crisp, approximately 10 minutes.
3. Meanwhile, beat egg slightly and mix in
   sugar, sour cream, horseradish, salt, and
   pepper. Stir in lemon juice very slowly.
4. Pour sauce over cooked cabbage, heat
   through, and serve hot.

FRENCH GREEN BEANS WITH
SUNFLOWER SEEDS

servings: 4   preparation time: 25 minutes

  1 pound green beans, tips removed
  6 tablespoons butter
½ cup sunflower seeds
salt and pepper to taste

1. Steam green beans until cooked yet firm.
2. In a large frying pan, melt butter over
   low heat.
3. Add beans, sunflower seeds, and
   seasoning. Increase to medium heat. Stir
   gently until beans are lightly browned.
   Serve immediately.

SQUASH PANCAKES

yield: 6–8 pancakes
preparation time: 25 minutes

1 large butternut or winter squash, peeled and
  grated
2 heaping tablespoons flour
2 eggs
salt and pepper to taste
oil

1. Mix all ingredients, except oil, together.
2. Wet hands. Roll batter into balls and
   flatten into cakes.
3. Carefully place each pancake into hot,
   deep oil.
4. Fry on medium heat for about 10 minutes
   on each side.
5. Place on paper towels to drain and
   serve hot.

MENU SUGGESTION

Serve with Fresh Asparagus Soup
(see page 43).

INDIAN PAKORA

servings: 4–6
preparation time: approximately 30 minutes

BATTER
  2 cups chick-pea flour
  1 teaspoon cumin
  1 teaspoon coriander
  ½ teaspoon cayenne
  salt to taste
  water, very cold

VEGETABLES (use no more than four
varieties at one meal):
carrots, sliced in ½-inch-wide, 1-inch-long
  strips
cauliflower, broken into small flowerlets
eggplant, sliced horizontally, ½ inch wide
green pepper, sliced in ½-inch-wide strips
potatoes, sliced very thin
spinach, coarsely chopped
zucchini, sliced horizontally, ½ inch wide

peanut oil
tamari sauce

1. Prepare batter by blending all ingredients
thoroughly.
2. Choose vegetables. Dip into batter and
coat well.
3. Pour at least three inches of oil into a
large frying pan, and fry vegetables, one
variety at a time, until golden brown.
(*Note:* Oil must be *very* hot—test by
dropping in a bit of batter. When batter
bubbles on contact, oil is ready.) Cooking
time will vary; carrots, eggplant, and
potatoes take longest.
4. Drain on paper towel and serve as quickly
as possible with tamari sauce on the side.

VARIATION

This dish is delicious accompanied by a bowl
of sauce made with two cups of sour cream
or yoghurt flavored with 1 minced garlic
clove and salt to taste.

MENU SUGGESTION

Serve with plain rice or Farina Side Dish
(see page 118).

MUSHROOM PIE

yield: 1 large or 2 small pies
preparation time: 1¾ hours

CRUST
2 cups pastry flour
¼ teaspoon salt
¼ pound butter
¼ cup (approximately) cold milk

FILLING
1 pound mushrooms, sliced
5 celery stalks, chopped
1 small onion, chopped
½ cup unsalted cashew nuts, chopped
pinch of thyme
salt and pepper to taste
4 tablespoons butter
Cream Sauce (see page 167)

1. Sift pastry flour with salt.
2. Prepare pie crust by cutting butter into flour first with two knives, then with fingers. Do not overmix; pastry dough should appear lumpy.
3. Add enough milk to hold dough together, blending mixture with a wooden spoon. Again: Do not overmix!
4. Divide dough into 2 balls (for a large pie) or into 4 balls (for 2 small pies). Chill pastry balls for approximately ½ hour.
5. While dough chills, prepare pie filling as follows: Sauté first 6 ingredients in 4 tablespoons butter, cover, and cook over low heat until mushrooms are tender.
6. Meanwhile, in a separate pan, make Cream Sauce (see page 167). Sauce should not be too thick; add more milk or cream if necessary.
7. Combine cooked mushroom mixture with Cream Sauce and blend well.
8. Preheat oven to 400°.
9. Roll out chilled dough balls on a floured board into circles approximately ¼ inch thick.
10. Grease a pie plate (or 2, if making small pies) and gently press 1 circle on bottom, reserving a strip of dough to place along edge of pie plate.
11. Pour in pie filling, then cover with another circle of dough. Fasten top layer of dough to bottom strip by pressing with fork tines. With a knife, make small slits evenly spaced around top layer to allow steam to escape while baking.
12. Reduce heat to 350° and bake in oven for ½ hour.
13. Allow to cool slightly before serving.

VARIATION

In place of mushrooms, substitute onions and grated Swiss (or Cheddar) cheese; or green peas. The filling variations are many, and great joy can be derived from experimenting.

MENU SUGGESTION

Serve with Mixed Fruit Salad (see page 33).

EASY VEGETABLE SUKIYAKI

servings: 4–6   preparation time: 20 minutes

  1 pound mushrooms, sliced
  2 tablespoons oil
  1 pound spinach, chopped
  3 celery stalks, diced
  2 cups bean sprouts
  1 can (6 ounces) bamboo shoots
¼ cup tamari sauce
  2 tablespoons Chinese brown sauce or
     molasses
¼ cup vegetable broth
salt and pepper to taste
  1 tablespoon cooking sherry (optional)

1. In a large deep frying pan or wok, heat
   oil and brown mushrooms.
2. Add remaining ingredients, stir well, and
   cook over medium heat for approximately
   10 minutes or until vegetables are tender
   yet slightly crisp. Serve immediately.

MENU SUGGESTION

Serve with Chinese Style Fried Rice
(see page 124).

BAKED STUFFED VEGETABLES

servings: 4
preparation time: varies with vegetable

1 large eggplant (or vegetable of your choice;
   see VARIATIONS)
melted butter or oil
4–6 tablespoons bread crumbs
grated Parmesan or Cheddar cheese
   (optional)

STUFFING
2 small onions, chopped fine
2 garlic cloves, minced
2 celery stalks, chopped fine
2 tablespoons chopped parsley
3 tablespoons butter or oil
1 cup bread crumbs or cooked rice
salt and pepper to taste

1. Steam eggplant until almost tender. Cut in half and remove pulp. Chop pulp and set aside to be used in stuffing.
2. Preheat oven to 350°.
3. Sauté onions, garlic, celery, and parsley in 3 tablespoons butter or oil for approximately 5 minutes.
4. Add remaining stuffing ingredients and chopped eggplant pulp and mix well.
5. Fill center of each eggplant half with stuffing. Top with bread crumbs and brush surface with melted butter or oil. Sprinkle with cheese (if desired).
6. Place stuffed eggplant halves in a casserole with approximately ¼ inch of water on bottom. Bake until brown and tender.

VARIATIONS

In place of eggplant, any one of the following vegetables can be used as described below:

ARTICHOKES (1 medium per serving): Steam until tender. Remove stems, bottom leaves, and about ¼ inch off tops. Chop stems and set aside for stuffing. Spread leaves apart and remove thistle. Fill center and rows between leaves with stuffing. Stuffing variation: Add capers and ¼ cup grated Parmesan cheese.

CAULIFLOWER (1 large): Steam until tender. Remove center stalk; chop and set aside for stuffing. Stuffing variation: Add tamari sauce, a dash of Tabasco sauce, and chopped toasted almonds.

PEPPERS (1 medium per serving): Cut slice from top and remove seeds. Steam until tender. Chop tops and set aside for stuffing. Stuffing variation: Substitute corn kernels for rice or bread crumbs, omit onions and celery, and add 2 cups grated Cheddar cheese. Mix 1 tablespoon flour with 2 tablespoons milk and a pinch of cayenne and combine with rest of ingredients.

ZUCCHINI (1 medium per serving): Follow directions for eggplant. Stuffing variations: Add oregano, pine nuts and ½ cup grated cheese; or raisins and chopped mint; or chopped tomatoes and cabbage leaves (cooked and chopped).

MENU SUGGESTION

Serve with lettuce salad with French Dressing (see page 166).

GREEK STUFFED GRAPE LEAVES

servings: 4   preparation time: 2 hours

20 canned or bottled grape leaves
    (best quality)
½ cup rice
water
  1 large onion, diced fine
  3 tablespoons butter
  1 teaspoon dill weed or fennel
  1 tablespoon chopped fresh mint or
    1 teaspoon dried mint
pinch of chili powder
salt and pepper to taste
½ cup roasted chick peas (optional)
½ cup currants
½ cup pine nuts

1. Rinse grape leaves well in hot water to remove brine. Set aside.
2. Parboil rice in ½ cup water until water is absorbed.
3. Meanwhile, sauté onions in butter until golden; then add rice and brown slightly. Add seasoning, chick peas, currants, and pine nuts. Remove from heat and allow to cool.
4. Place a teaspoonful of mixture in center of each grape leaf and roll fairly tightly, starting at the stem end and turning in the sides so that filling is securely wrapped. Use all of filling; any left over can be frozen.
5. Pack leaves into a pan, layer upon layer, and barely cover with water. Press a plate on top of leaves to prevent them from falling apart, and cover pan. Cook slowly for approximately 1½ hours—checking from time to time that some water remains on bottom of pan to prevent leaves from sticking or burning—until rice is cooked yet firm. Serve either hot or cold with a large bowl of yoghurt or sour cream.

NOTE

Any extra grape leaves may be stored in a jar, covered with brine or water, and kept in the refrigerator for future stuffing.

MENU SUGGESTION

Serve with Cold Quick "Real" Borscht (see page 50).

EGG ROLLS

yield: 16–20 egg rolls
preparation time: 30 minutes

WRAPPING
   2 cups pastry flour
   2 eggs
2¾ cups water

FILLING
   4 tablespoons peanut oil
   2 tablespoons tamari sauce
   3 scallions, sliced fine
   2 cups shredded bean sprouts
   2 cups shredded cabbage
½ cup toasted sesame seeds
salt to taste
   1 teaspoon sugar (optional)

cornstarch
water
peanut oil

1. Beat wrapping ingredients together until smooth.
2. Lightly grease a small frying pan. Pour in 1 ladleful of batter and tilt pan until batter covers bottom entirely. Allow a thin layer to adhere to bottom and quickly pour excess back into bowl. Cook on one side for approximately 1 minute. Flip onto a plate, fried side up. Repeat process until all batter is used.
3. In a large pan, heat oil and tamari sauce. Add remaining filling ingredients and stir well until tender yet crisp, approximately 3 minutes.
4. Place approximately 2 tablespoons of filling on lower half of wrapping, fold in sides, and roll tightly. Make a paste with a little cornstarch and water; brush along ends, press, and seal. Continue until all filling is used.
5. In hot peanut oil, deep-fry egg rolls until well browned on all sides. Drain on paper towels. Serve hot or cold.

NOTE

Any leftover wrappings can be deep fried and eaten like potato chips.

chapter 5
GRAINS, RICE, AND DRIED BEANS

Rice, whole grains and beans are all marvelous sources of energy and can be served frequently as filling main courses.

The rice you use should be brown rice, either short or long grain. White rice, because of the polishing and processing it undergoes, lacks flavor and food value (and is also more fattening!). Brown rice is simple to cook; the main difference is that it takes a little longer. Here are two basic ways to cook it:

BOILED. Put one part rice in a strainer or colander and wash thoroughly with cold water. Place rice in a heavy pot with two parts water and some salt. Bring water to a boil and boil rapidly until water is absorbed to about ½ inch above rice. Cover tightly, lower heat and cook slowly for at least 45 minutes or until rice is tender yet firm. Add more water if necessary. *Note:* If you prefer, rice may be boiled without being washed; add more water.

SAUTEED AND STEAMED. Heat a small amount of oil or butter in a heavy pot, sauté one part rice lightly, stirring constantly, until toasted. Add two parts boiling water, cover tightly, lower heat and cook slowly for at least 45 minutes or until rice is tender yet firm. Add more water if necessary. *Note:* Onions, mushrooms, or other vegetables may be sautéed and steamed together with the rice.

A wide range of menus is made possible by the variety of whole grains available. In many recipes the grains specified can be interchanged with rice or another grain. Some of the grains most commonly used are bulgur, barley (hulled and unpearled), millet, buckwheat groats (kasha) and wheat berry (wheat grain, green corn).

A basic way to cook most grains is the sautéing-and-steaming method used for rice (see above).

Important: Never stir rice or grains once the water is boiling, as this will cause them to stick.

Dried beans and peas are delicious and versatile either alone or with rice or grains. There are many different kinds: lima (large and baby), navy, marrow, small white, pinto, kidney, lentil, soybeans; split peas (green and yellow), black-eyed peas, chick peas (ceci, garbanzos), etc. Most dried beans need at least 6 hours to soak and at least double in volume when soaked; 2 cups of dried beans will generally serve 6 people. Soaked beans may be stored in the refrigerator for later use.

Cook beans in the water in which they were soaked; use bean water in sauces, soups etc. When puréeing beans, do so while they are still warm and use some of the cooking liquid.

Vegetable broth may be substituted for water in all rice, grain and bean recipes.

Yoghurt is a delicious accompaniment to many grain and bean dishes.

BAKED BARLEY AND MUSHROOMS

servings: 4   preparation time: 1½ hours

   1 onion, diced
½ pound mushrooms, sliced
   1 cup barley
salt and pepper to taste
   5 tablespoons butter
2½ cups vegetable broth, boiling

1. Preheat oven to 350°.
2. In a large deep frying pan, sauté onion, mushrooms, barley, and seasoning in butter. Stir frequently until barley is lightly browned.
3. Place in a casserole and stir in broth.
4. Cover and bake for approximately 1 hour. If barley is too firm when all the liquid is absorbed, add additional boiling water. However, avoid overcooking—barley is more delicious when firm and slightly crunchy.

NOTE

Be very careful when removing cover from casserole, as steam builds up within.

MENU SUGGESTION

Serve with All-Green-Vegetable Soup (see page 45).

FARINA SIDE DISH

servings: 4   preparation time: 30 minutes

2 potatoes, peeled and diced small
1 cup water
½ cup oil
2 cups farina
salt and pepper to taste

1. Boil potatoes in salted water.
2. Meanwhile, heat oil, add farina, and sauté over low heat. Stir constantly until farina is golden brown.
3. Mash potatoes in cooking water and add seasoning.
4. Add sautéed farina to mashed potatoes. Mix well, cover, and cook over low heat until farina is tender. Serve hot.

NOTE

When finished, this dish should resemble fine egg barley.

WHEAT BERRY
IN HAZELNUT-LEEK SAUCE

servings: 4–6   preparation time: 1 hour

2 cups wheat berry
2 tablespoons oil
water
½ cup chopped hazelnuts
3 garlic cloves, minced
2 leeks, cut in ½-inch pieces
salt to taste

1. In a large frying pan, toast grain in
   1 tablespoon oil, moving pan constantly,
   until grain begins to pop.
2. Add water to a level approximately 1 inch
   above grain and boil over low heat,
   uncovered, for approximately 45 minutes,
   or until tender. Add more boiling water if
   necessary.
3. Meanwhile, sauté nuts, garlic, leeks, and
   salt in remaining oil. Add about 1
   tablespoon water, cover tightly and steam
   over low heat for approximately 20 minutes,
   or until water is absorbed.
4. When grain is tender, transfer to a
   casserole, spoon nut-leek sauce on top,
   and cover. Steam in a warm (300°) oven for
   approximately 15 minutes before serving.

NOTE

As grains vary, test to see if more water
is needed. When cooked, grain should be firm
and slightly crunchy.

MENU SUGGESTION

Serve with Many-Vegetable Salad
(see page 32).

COUSCOUS WITH VEGETABLES

servings: 4   preparation time: 2 hours
                     (not including soaking)

1 cup chick peas, soaked 6 hours, or 2 cups
  cooked chick peas
1 pound couscous (a wheat cereal resembling
  semolina which can be purchased, boxed,
  in Near Eastern and natural food stores).
1 pound yellow or butternut squash, or
  pumpkin, cut in chunks
3 green peppers, cut in quarters
1 turnip, cut in chunks
2 celery stalks, cut in chunks
1 onion, cut in chunks
3 tomatoes, cut in chunks (optional)
1 teaspoon salt
1 teaspoon paprika (sharp)
1 pinch of cumin seed
2 cloves

GARNISH (optional)
  6 onions or leeks, sliced
Oil
½ cup blanched almonds
½ cup raisins
pinch of saffron powder
  1 teaspoon cinnamon

1. If using soaked chick peas, drain, reserve
   liquid, and boil over low heat until
   tender, approximately 1 hour.
2. Put couscous in a bowl, pour some hot
   water over it, and allow to stand for

10 minutes, until water is absorbed.
3. Using a special couscous pot (see NOTE)
   pour into lower pot the reserved water
   from chick peas—or liquid from canned
   cooked chick peas—and additional water
   to make 3 quarts altogether. Bring to a boil.
4. Place vegetables, chick peas, and
   seasoning in boiling water; put couscous in
   upper pot, cover, and steam for 15 minutes.
5. Meanwhile, make garnish, if desired, by
   browning onions in oil, adding remaining
   ingredients and cooking, covered, for
   15 minutes.
6. Transfer couscous to a bowl, add two
   ladlefuls of cooking liquid, and stir well.
7. Return couscous to upper pot, cover, and
   steam for another 15 minutes.
8. Place couscous on a platter, spoon
   vegetables on top and pour liquid from
   lower pot over them. Serve with the bowl
   of onion garnish.

NOTE

A couscous pot is a double pot. The upper
pot is perforated and fits into the lower pot—
much like a double-boiler—but the
perforations allow the steam to come
through to cook and flavor the couscous.
It might be possible to improvise a similar
kind of pot, but the actual couscous pot
is best to use for this dish.

BUCKWHEAT GROATS (KASHA) WITH MUSHROOM SAUCE

servings: 4–6   preparation time: 30 minutes

1 small onion, chopped fine
3 tablespoons oil
2 cups buckwheat groats
1 egg, beaten well
salt and pepper to taste
vegetable broth, boiling

SAUCE

½ pound mushrooms, sliced
2 tablespoons butter
Brown Sauce (see page 168), double recipe

1. In a large pot, sauté onion lightly in oil.
2. Mix groats and egg together well. Add salt and pepper.
3. Toast groats mixture in oil, stirring constantly with a wooden spoon until groats are browned, separated, and dry.
4. Gradually add vegetable broth to approximately ½ inch above groats. Lower heat, cover, and cook until broth is absorbed. If groats are too firm, add more broth or boiling water.
5. In a small pan, sauté mushrooms in butter until tender. Combine Brown Sauce (made with onion) with cooked mushrooms and mix well with groats. Heat through and serve hot.

MENU SUGGESTION

Serve with asparagus with Green Sauce (see page 164).

BAKED RICE AND VEGETABLES

servings: 4   preparation time: 2 hours

  2 cups rice
  2 tablespoons oil
  4 carrots or 1 yellow squash, cut in chunks
  6 small whole onions or 2 large onions,
     cut in chunks
  ½ cabbage or 2 turnips or 2 white radishes,
     cut in chunks
  3 garlic cloves, chopped
  2 tablespoons tamari sauce
water
salt to taste

1. In a large heavy pot, toast rice in oil until lightly browned, stirring constantly with a wooden spoon.
2. Place vegetables over rice.
3. Combine water, tamari sauce, and salt; pour to a level approximately 1 inch above vegetables.
4. Tightly cover pot and bake in 350° oven for approximately 1½ hours, or until water is absorbed. If rice is too firm, add more water; cover and continue baking until tender. Serve hot.

VARIATION

Barley, kasha, or wheat berry can be substituted for the rice. Adjust amount of water to the type of grain used.

CHINESE-STYLE FRIED RICE

servings: 2   preparation time: 10 minutes

3 tablespoons oil
2 scallions, diced
1 celery stalk, diced
2 cups rice, cooked
2 eggs
4 tablespoons milk
1 tablespoon tamari sauce
pinch of nutmeg
2 tablespoons chopped parsley

1. In a large frying pan or wok, heat oil.
   Sauté scallions and celery until golden.
2. Add rice, stirring constantly with a wooden
   spoon, and fry for approximately
   5 minutes.
3. Beat egg with milk, tamari sauce, and
   seasoning.
4. Pour egg mixture into rice and stir over
   medium heat until eggs set. Serve hot.

NOTE
This dish is enhanced if left in a warm oven
for a few minutes before serving.

CUBAN RICE

servings: 4–6   preparation time: 1 hour

  2 cups rice
  4 onions
¼ cup olive oil
  4 garlic cloves, minced
  3 green peppers, sliced
  5 tomatoes, peeled, seeded, and cubed
  1 teaspoon oregano
½ teaspoon crushed, hot red pepper
    (optional)
salt and pepper to taste
½ pound mushrooms, sliced

1. Cook rice until tender.
2. Meanwhile, in a large frying pan, sauté
   onions in oil until golden.
3. Add garlic and brown slightly.
4. Add peppers, tomatoes, and seasoning;
   reduce heat, cover, and simmer.
5. In a separate pan, sauté mushrooms in a
   little oil.
6. When all vegetables are tender, combine
   them. Serve hot over rice.

FANCY PERSIAN RICE

servings: 6–8   preparation time: 1½ hours

    4 cups long-grain rice
    3 potatoes, peeled and sliced thin
⅓ cup raisins or ½ cup currants, soaked
      in water and drained
⅛ teaspoon saffron, soaked in ¼ cup
      hot water
4 tablespoons butter
salt to taste

1. Rinse rice and boil in salted water. When
   tender but still firm, rinse again in cold
   water to separate grains.
2. Preheat oven to 350°.
3. Grease bottom of casserole and cover with
   raw potato slices. Dot with lumps of butter
   and spread rice evenly on top. Sprinkle
   with raisins or currants and saffron water.
4. Melt remaining butter and pour over rice.
5. Cover and steam in oven for approximately
   15 minutes.
6. Remove from oven, shake gently from
   side to side, and allow to stand, uncovered,
   for 10 minutes.
7. Transfer to serving dish and discard
   potatoes. Serve warm.

MENU SUGGESTION

Serve with a large bowl of stewed prunes
or plums and lettuce salad with Miso and
Tahini Sauce (see page 169).

VEGETABLE PAELLA

servings: 4   preparation time: 1 hour

2 cups rice
5 cups water
2 onions, sliced fine
4 garlic cloves, minced
2 large or 4 small green peppers, sliced thin
1 large tomato, sliced
3 tablespoons olive oil
1 bay leaf
1 teaspoon powdered saffron
salt to taste
1 cup peas, cooked
4 pimientos, diced

1. Boil rice in 2½ cups salted water, covered, until water is absorbed.
2. Meanwhile, in a large pot, brown onions, garlic, peppers, and tomato in oil.
3. Mix rice with vegetables and add remaining water and seasoning. Cover and cook over low heat until water is nearly absorbed.
4. Add peas and pimientos. Do not stir. Check to see if rice is tender—if necessary add boiling water. Serve hot.

MENU SUGGESTION

Serve with spinach salad and Tahini Dressing (see page 165).

SOYBEANS AND MUSHROOMS

servings: 4   preparation time: 25 minutes

½ onion, diced
 1 garlic clove, minced
 3 tablespoons butter
½ pound mushrooms, sliced
salt and pepper to taste
 1 tablespoon tamari sauce
 1 tablespoon molasses or Chinese brown
    sauce
 2 cups soybeans, cooked
 1 tablespoon chopped fresh dill
    or 1 teaspoon dill weed

1. Sauté onion and garlic in butter until
   golden.
2. Add mushrooms, salt, and pepper. Cover
   and sauté over low heat until mushrooms
   are tender.
3. In a separate pan combine tamari and
   molasses or brown sauce. Blend well and
   add soybeans. Cover and cook over low
   heat for approximately 10 minutes.
4. Combine soybean mixture with mushrooms
   and stir well. Top with dill and serve
   immediately.

MENU SUGGESTION

Serve with buttered noodles or macaroni.

BULENT'S CHICK PEAS

servings: 4   preparation time: 30 minutes
                (not including soaking)

2 small onions, diced
1 tomato, peeled, seeded, and diced
3 tablespoons olive oil
1 cup dried chick peas, soaked 6 hours
pinch of thyme, basil, oregano, and salt

1. Cook chick peas until almost tender.
2. Sauté onions and tomato in olive oil until
   tender.
3. Add chick peas and herbs. Cover and
   sauté over low heat until chick peas are
   tender.

MENU SUGGESTION

Serve with rice cooked with pine nuts and
Chilled Zucchini (see page 89).

"HOT" BEANS AND SPINACH

servings: 6   preparation time: 45 minutes
            (not including soaking)

2 cups dried white or pinto beans, soaked
  6 hours
2 tablespoons vegetable or peanut oil
2 garlic cloves, minced
1 pound spinach, chopped
1 hot red pepper, diced
salt and pepper to taste
pinch of cayenne

1. Cook beans over low heat until tender.
   Reserve 1 cup cooking liquid before
   draining.
2. In a deep frying pan, sauté garlic in oil.
3. Add spinach and stir for approximately
   5 minutes.
4. Add beans, red pepper, and seasoning.
   Stir thoroughly over high heat until beans
   are lightly browned. Then add cooking
   water, lower heat, cover, and cook for
   approximately 20 minutes, until all flavors
   are well blended. Serve hot.

NOTE

This dish should be saucelike, so add a bit
more water if beans begin to dry out during
cooking.

MENU SUGGESTION

Serve with rice with Tamari and Tahini Sauce
(see page 169).

HOT LENTIL PÂTE

servings: 4   preparation time: 1½ hours

1½ cups lentils
  2 tablespoons oil
  2 small onions, diced
  1 garlic clove—minced
 ½ cup chopped parsley
  2 small hard rolls or 3 slices hard bread,
    soaked in water
pinch each of thyme, coriander, celery seed,
    and chili powder
  2 tablespoons chopped fresh dill or
    1 tablespoon dill weed
salt and pepper to taste
  1 egg, beaten
juice of ½ lemon
dash of tamari sauce

1. Wash lentils well and boil slowly for approximately 40 minutes, or until tender.
2. Meanwhile, sauté onions, garlic, and parsley in oil. Squeeze out excess water from rolls or bread and add to onion mixture. Add seasoning. Stir well over medium heat for 10 minutes, adding water if necessary (mixture should be fairly moist).
3. Preheat oven to 350°.
4. Mash lentils in a food mill or blender.
5. Combine lentils with onion mixture, egg, lemon juice, and tamari sauce; mix well. Mixture should have a heavy consistency.
6. Bake in a greased pan for ½ hour, or until bottom is well browned. Serve hot or cold.

MENU SUGGESTION

Serve with Brussels Sprouts, Water Chestnuts, and Mushrooms (see page 95).

DRIED BEANS WITH GARLIC SAUCE

servings: 4   preparation time: 1½ hours
(not including soaking)

1 pound white or black beans, soaked
  6 hours
1 head garlic, whole
1 garlic clove, minced
½ cup olive oil
1 teaspoon cumin
1 tablespoon salt

1. Peel outer covering of garlic but leave
   cluster whole.
2. Cover beans and garlic with water and
   cook, uncovered, until beans are almost
   tender.
3. Drain and remove garlic. Place beans in a
   bean pot or suitable pan.
4. In a small frying pan, sauté minced garlic
   clove in oil until yellow. Strain and combine
   oil with cumin and salt.
5. Pour oil mixture onto beans and cook,
   uncovered, for approximately 25 minutes.
   Serve hot.

MENU SUGGESTION

Serve with Farina Side Dish (see page 118).

MIDDLE EASTERN LIMA BEANS

servings: 6   preparation time: 2½ hours
(not including soaking)

2 cups dried lima beans, soaked 6 hours
8 cups salted water
3 tablespoons butter
2 onions, chopped
¼ teaspoon turmeric
½ teaspoon powdered cloves
salt and pepper to taste
1 large tart apple, cored and chopped

1. Drain beans, place in a large pot, and cover with salted water. Boil until tender, approximately 1½–2 hours.
2. Drain, but reserve cooking water.
3. In a large frying pan or pot, heat butter and sauté onions until golden. Add seasoning and apple. Stir well and simmer until apple is cooked.
4. Add cooked beans and enough of the cooking water to moisten. Cook slowly for 8–10 minutes. Serve hot.

MENU SUGGESTION

Serve with rice, bulgur, or millet in Brown Sauce (with mushrooms) (see page 168).

chapter 6
SANDWICHES, APPETIZERS, AND HORS D'OEUVRES

I think you will be surprised at all the types of sandwiches and appetizers that may be made to replace (or augment) the old standbys.

Vegetable or bean spreads make good sandwich fillings; a large quantity can be prepared at one time and stored in the refrigerator. Make free use of the many nut butters available, such as peanut, cashew, sesame and almond. They are delicious alone or in combination with other ingredients.

Again—invent, experiment and enjoy the results!

EGG AND AVOCADO SPREAD

servings: 4   preparation time: 10 minutes
(not including chilling)

1 large ripe avocado
4 hard-cooked eggs
1 tablespoon mayonnaise (approximately)
½ large or 1 small onion, chopped fine
½ large or 1 small apple, chopped fine
pinch each of mustard powder and garlic salt
salt and pepper to taste

1. Mash avocado and eggs well.
2. Add remaining ingredients and mix well.
   Chill and use as a sandwich spread.

NOTE

Stored in a tight container, this spread keeps
well in the refrigerator for future use.

VARIATION

To use as a dip, increase the amount of
mayonnaise.

EGGPLANT SPREAD

servings: 4   preparation time: 40 minutes
(not including chilling)

       1 large eggplant
       1 onion, chopped
       1 green pepper, chopped
   1½ tablespoons olive oil
       1 large apple, peeled and cored
       2 hard-cooked eggs (optional)
       1 tablespoon lemon juice
     12 black olives, pitted and chopped fine
     ½ teaspoon sugar
salt to taste
pinch of chili powder

1. Bake eggplant in 350° oven until very soft.
2. Meanwhile, sauté onion and green pepper
   lightly in ½ tablespoon oil. Allow to cool.
3. Grate apple and eggs together.
4. Remove skin and seeds from eggplant;
   drain well and mash until fluffy.
5. Combine all ingredients. Mix well and chill.
   Use as a sandwich spread, or serve as an
   appetizer on lettuce.

NOTE

Omit eggs if spread is to be refrigerated for
a lengthy period.

GUACAMOLE

servings: 2   preparation time: 5 minutes
(not including chilling)

salt to taste
1 garlic clove, cut in half
1 large ripe avocado
½ onion, chopped fine
½ teaspoon chili powder
¼ teaspoon mustard powder
1 teaspoon lemon juice
mayonnaise

1. Sprinkle salt in a bowl and rub in garlic.
2. Mash avocado well and combine with remaining ingredients, except mayonnaise.
3. Spread a layer of mayonnaise on top and chill. Blend in mayonnaise just before serving. Use as a sandwich spread or serve as an appetizer on lettuce.

MUSHROOM AND CELERY APPETIZER

servings: 4   preparation time: 5 minutes
(not including chilling)

½ pound whole small mushrooms or large
  mushroom caps
4 stalks celery, cut in large chunks
1 small jar capers, drained
4 tablespoons olive oil
1½ tablespoons cider vinegar
pinch of thyme

1. Blanch mushrooms and celery by stirring
   in boiling water for approximately 2
   minutes (blanching keeps mushrooms
   white). Remove quickly from water.
2. Combine with all remaining ingredients
   and mix well. Chill and serve with
   crackers or flat bread.

VARIATION

This dish can become a mealtime salad by
increasing the amounts of mushrooms and
celery.

VEGETABLE PÂTÉ

yield: canapés for 10, or 4 sandwiches
preparation time: 30 minutes (not including
  chilling)

½ pound butter
2 yellow onions, chopped
4 small white onions (or 1 large Bermuda
  onion), chopped
½ pound shallots, sliced
2 garlic cloves, minced
1 pound mushrooms, sliced
pinch each of coriander, cardamom, and
  pepper
½ teaspoon curry powder
salt to taste
bunch of fresh dill, chopped

1. Using half the butter, sauté onions, shallots,
   and garlic over medium heat until pale
   yellow.
2. Add mushrooms, seasoning (except dill),
   and remaining butter. Lower heat, cover,
   and sauté until mushrooms are tender.
3. Remove from heat and allow to cool
   slightly; then place in blender and purée.
4. Transfer to a bowl or dish, top with dill,
   and chill until ready to serve.
5. Serve with crackers or flat bread; or, with
   lettuce, as a sandwich spread.

NOTE

Pâté will keep well for several days when
stored in a tight container and refrigerated.

CREAM CHEESE AND APPLE SANDWICH

Between two slices of whole-wheat or corn bread, place a layer each of cream cheese, wafer-thin apple slices, and chopped walnuts or almonds. Top with a few sprigs of watercress or fresh mint.

CHEDDAR-AVOCADO-SPROUTS SANDWICH

Spread nut butter on a slice of whole-wheat bread. Place on top: 2 thin slices each of avocado and tomato and a thick slice of sharp Cheddar cheese. Melt butter in a pan and grill, covered, over low heat until cheese melts. Sprinkle liberally with alfalfa sprouts and serve hot with a fork and knife.

COLD ASPARAGUS SANDWICH

Between two slices of whole-wheat or homemade white bread, place cold cooked asparagus, Russian dressing, a few slices of pimiento, and a sprinkling of toasted sesame seeds.

CHICK-PEA SPREAD (HUMUS)

servings: 4   preparation time: 5 minutes

1 cup chick peas, cooked
1 cup tahini (sesame butter)
2 tablespoons olive oil
juice of 2 lemons
2 garlic cloves, pressed
salt to taste
chopped parsley

1. Mash chick peas well in a blender or
   food mill.
2. Combine with remaining ingredients,
   except parsley, and mix well. Spread on
   bread or crackers, or serve as an appetizer
   on lettuce. Garnish with parsley.

NOTE

To use as a dip, increase the amount of
olive oil, or add water.

chapter 7
BREADS, CAKES, AND COOKIES

Use stone-ground whole-grain flours whenever possible. Try to avoid enriched white flour and replace it with whole-wheat, corn, rye, soy, oatmeal, wheat germ or combinations of them. Whole-wheat pastry flour can be obtained for baking requiring finer flour.

Here are some hints for adapting white flour recipes to whole-wheat:

1. Sift flour at least 3 times.
2. One cup of white flour equals ¾ cup of whole-wheat flour.
3. Whole-wheat flour requires more liquid (approximately ¼ more) and slightly less oil, depending upon the texture.
4. Replace white sugar with honey or molasses (use ⅔ quantity called for). Whole-wheat flours vary, so adjust amounts according to the type being used.

CHAPATTIS (INDIAN FLAT BREAD)

yield: 8 large chapattis
preparation time: 15 minutes.

2 cups whole-wheat flour
1 teaspoon salt
2 tablespoons toasted sesame seeds
water

1. Mix dry ingredients together.
2. Pour in enough water to make dough
   pliable and knead well. Add just enough
   water for dough to have skinlike texture
   and continue kneading, roughly, until
   dough is a smooth and elastic ball.
3. Pinch off a small piece of dough, form
   into a small ball, and roll continuously on
   a floured board into a very thin circle
   of dough. Repeat until all dough is used.
4. Heat a griddle or frying pan very hot.
   Put chapatti on for approximately ½ minute
   on each side. (Dough "blisters" slightly
   and brown marks appear.)
5. Flip onto warmed plate—cover with cloth
   to keep warm—and repeat process until all
   chapattis are cooked.
6. Butter lightly and serve.

RYE BREAD

yield: 2 loaves   preparation time: 3½ hours

  2 envelopes (1 ounce) dry yeast
½ cup warm water
  1 tablespoon salt
  3 tablespoons caraway seeds
½ cup molasses (light)
  1 cup warm water
  2 tablespoons vegetable or seed oil
  2 cups all-purpose flour, sifted
  3 cups rye flour, sifted
oil

1. Mix yeast in ½ cup warm water to soften.
2. Combine salt, caraway seeds, molasses, remaining water, and 2 tablespoons oil; and add yeast.
3. Mix flours and slowly stir into yeast mixture. Knead dough on floured board until very smooth. Form into a ball and place in a greased bowl. Brush with oil, cover, and place bowl in a warm place. Allow to stand until doubled in size, approximately 1½ hours.
4. Punch down dough and form into a ball again. Cover and allow to stand for 10 minutes.
5. Form into two loaves. Place loaves in greased bread pans. Cover again and allow to rise until doubled in size, approximately 1 hour.
6. Preheat oven to 450°.
7. Brush loaves lightly with water or egg yolk and bake for 10 min. Lower heat to 350° and bake ½ hour longer.
8. Allow crust to become brown, and then cover with foil or paper to prevent burning.

MATZO MEAL DUMPLINGS

yield: about 30 dumplings
preparation time: 30 minutes

    5 potatoes, cooked, peeled, and mashed
    5 eggs
    5 teaspoons salt
1¼ cup oil
1¼ cup matzo meal

1. Mix all ingredients together thoroughly.
2. Form into balls the size of a small egg.
3. Drop balls into boiling salted water. Cook until dumplings expand and float to the surface, approximately 20 minutes.
4. Serve in any clear or puréed vegetable soup.

NOTE

Dumpling mixture can be kept in refrigerator, covered, until ready to cook.

UNYEASTED WHOLE-WHEAT BREAD WITH FRUIT AND NUTS

yield: 1 large or 2 small loaves
preparation time: 1½ hours

 3 cups whole-wheat flour
 1 cup corn flour
½ cup chopped hazelnuts
½ cup chopped raisins
 1 teaspoon salt
 2 teaspoons cinnamon
 1 egg yolk
 1 cup water (approximately)

1. Preheat oven to 350°.
2. Mix all ingredients (except water) together with hands.
3. Add water slowly and knead well until dough is smooth and has skinlike texture. Add more water if necessary.
4. Shape into loaf or loaves, brush a bit of egg yolk or water on top, and place in a greased pan or on a cookie sheet. Bake for approximately 1 hour.

VARIATIONS

With carrots: Use same ingredients and procedure as above, but omit fruit, nuts, and cinnamon and substitute two carrots cut into "matchsticks" (see page 101) and sautéed in 1 teaspoon oil.

With onions: Use same ingredients and procedure as in first variation, but omit carrots and substitute two onions, sliced and sautéed in 1 teaspoon oil.

CARROT TORTE

yield: 1 10-inch torte
preparation time: 1 hour

12 eggs, separated
¾ cup sugar
 6 tablespoons grated carrot
 6 tablespoons grated apple
 6 tablespoons grated almonds
 3 tablespoons flour
 1 teaspoon lemon juice
pinch of salt

1. Preheat oven to 375°.
2. Mix egg yolks and sugar together until pale yellow. Add apple, carrot, and almonds. Fold in flour. Add lemon juice.
3. Whip egg whites and salt stiff, and fold into batter.
4. Grease a 10-inch cake pan (spring form, if possible) and sprinkle with a little flour or wheat germ. Pour in batter and bake until an inserted knife comes out dry, approximately 45 minutes.

MATZO MEAL ROLLS

yield: 12 rolls   preparation time: 1 hour

1½ cups water
 ½ cup vegetable or seed oil
 2 teaspoons sugar
 ½ teaspoon salt
 2 cups matzo meal
 5 eggs

1. Preheat oven to 450°.
2. Combine water, oil, sugar, and salt and bring to a boil.
3. Remove from heat and immediately add matzo meal, beating well.
4. Allow mixture to cool; then add eggs, one at a time, beating continuously.
5. Grease a cookie sheet well. Drop on mixture by tablespoonfuls.
6. Bake at 450° for 10 minutes, then lower oven to 350° and bake for an additional 25 minutes. These rolls taste best when served warm.

BASIC WHOLE-WHEAT BREAD

yield: 2 loaves   preparation time: 2 hours

  7 cups whole-wheat flour
  1 tablespoon salt
½ cup warm water
  1 tablespoon honey or molasses
  2 envelopes (1 ounce) dry yeast
  2 cups warm water

1. Mix flour and salt in a large bowl.
2. Heat oven to about 200° and put bowl in, leaving oven-door open, for approximately 10 minutes.
3. Meanwhile, mix yeast, ½ cup warm water, and honey in a bowl; keep warm on top of stove for 15 minutes.
4. Grease 2 cookie sheets or baking pans.
5. Take flour from oven and stir in yeast mixture (which should be bubbly). Gradually stir in 2 cups of warm water, and knead 5–10 minutes.
6. Shape into two loaves and place on cookie sheets or in bread pans.
7. Place on top shelf of warm oven, half-closing door, and allow to rise for approximately 20 minutes.
8. Increase heat to 375°, close door, and bake for 45 minutes.
9. At the end of baking time, tap bottoms of loaves. If they sound hollow, they are done. Bake a few minutes more if not done.
10. Cool loaves on rack.

VARIATION

1 cup raisins may be added before baking.

SUNFLOWER MEAL COOKIES

yield: about 14 cookies
preparation time: 40 minutes

¾ cup sunflower meal
¼ cup wheat germ
 2 tablespoons honey
 2 tablespoons oil (preferably safflower)
 1 egg, beaten well
½ tart apple, grated
pinch of salt
1. Preheat oven to 350°.
2. Mix all ingredients together well with
   beater or wooden spoon.
3. Grease a cookie sheet and drop batter
   by tablespoonfuls.
4. Bake for ½ hour. Remove from sheet and
   allow to cool before serving.

FRUIT AND NUT CAKE

yield: 1 9-inch cake   preparation time: 1 hour

  1 ¾ cup flour
  1 teaspoon baking soda
½ teaspoon salt
  1 teaspoon cinnamon
½ teaspoon nutmeg
½ cup honey
¼ cup peanut oil
  1 egg, beaten
  1 cup toasted and chopped almonds
  1 cup chopped raisins
  1 cup applesauce, warm

1. Preheat oven to 350°.
2. Sift flour, soda, salt, cinnamon, and
   nutmeg together.
3. In a separate bowl, blend honey and oil
   well; then beat in egg.
4. Stir dry ingredients into honey and oil
   mixture gradually, and beat until smooth.
5. Add nuts, raisins, and applesauce;
   beat well.
6. Pour batter into greased 9-inch tube pan
   and bake for aproximately 40 minutes, or
   until knife inserted in center comes out
   clean.

VARIATIONS

Try experimenting with other fruits and nuts
such as apricots, oranges, dates, and walnuts.

JELLY ROLL

yield: 1 roll   preparation time: 30 minutes

  4 eggs, separated
½ teaspoon salt
  1 cup sugar
  1 teaspoon baking powder
  1 cup flour
  1 teaspoon almond or vanilla extract
jam or jelly

1. Preheat oven to 375°.
2. Whip egg whites with half of salt until
   almost stiff; then fold in sugar.
3. Beat egg yolks with remaining salt until
   pale yellow and add to egg whites mixture.
4. Sift other dry ingredients together into
   mixture, add flavoring, and mix well.
5. Line a jelly roll pan with aluminum foil.
   Pour in mixture evenly and bake for
   approximately 15 minutes.
6. Remove from oven and carefully strip off
   foil. Place cake right side up on waxed
   paper, spread with jam or jelly, and roll
   into a log.
7. Place waxed paper around log until set.

VARIATION

Ice cream may also be used as filling:
Roll cake in wax paper and, when cool, unroll
and fill with ice cream. Place in freezer
until ready to serve.

MOTHER'S BUTTER COOKIES

yield: 80 cookies
preparation time: 1½ hours (including chilling)

```
½ pound butter, at room temperature
 1 cup sugar
 2 egg yolks
3¾ cups flour
 1 teaspoon baking powder (optional)
½ teaspoon salt
 1 lemon, juice and grated rind
```

1. Cream butter well with sugar.
2. Beat in egg yolks and remaining ingredients.
3. Form dough into roll about 1½ inches in diameter. Wrap roll in waxed paper and chill ½–1 hour.
4. Heat oven to 450°.
5. Cut roll into ¼-inch slices. Place on ungreased cookie sheet and bake for 10–12 minutes. Remove while still warm.

VARIATIONS

Dough can be cut with a cookie press after chilling. For fancier cookies, top with ground nuts and sugar or, when done, ice with water frosting and sprinkles.

chapter 8
SAUCES AND DRESSINGS

Sauces and dressings can transform simple vegetables and salads into gourmet masterpieces. There are many sauces and dressings that can be adapted to vegetarian cookery. The few I have chosen for inclusion here are generally made from natural ingredients and are quick and easy to prepare.

Sauces and dressings are greatly enhanced by the addition of seeds, nuts and herbs. Check with A Glossary of Herbs (pages 17–19) to find out which herb goes best with which fruit or vegetable. Egg yolks are a delicious rich thickener for sauces.

Try to be discriminating when using sauces. If your dishes are made from good quality wholesome ingredients, the sauces should be used as a complement and not as a disguise.

MUSTARD-HONEY SALAD DRESSING

yield: ½ cup   preparation time: 5 minutes

4 tablespoons olive oil
3 tablespoons lemon juice or vinegar
1 tablespoon honey
1 teaspoon mustard powder diluted with
   1 teaspoon cold water
1 garlic clove, pressed
salt and pepper to taste

Combine all ingredients and blend well.

GREEN SAUCE

yield: 1½ cups   preparation time: 5 minutes

½ cup olive or seed oil
¼ cup vinegar
pinch of mustard powder
  2 hard-cooked eggs, whites chopped,
    yolks mashed
  3 shallots, chopped fine
  2 tablespoons coarsely chopped capers
¼ cup chopped mixed fresh green herbs:
    basil, mint, tarragon, thyme, dill
¼ cup chopped parsley

Blend or shake all ingredients well and chill.
Serve over cooked asparagus or as a
salad dressing.

TOMATO SAUCE

yield: 4 cups   preparation time: 2½ hours

2 large onions, diced
2 stalks celery, diced
1 green pepper, diced
1 garlic clove, minced
2 tablespoons olive oil
4 large ripe tomatoes, cut in large chunks,
   or 1 large can tomatoes
1 can tomato paste
1 cup water (approximately)
1 teaspoon oregano
¼ teaspoon sweet basil
1 tablespoon sugar
salt and pepper to taste
¼ cup grated Parmesan cheese (optional)

1. In a large frying pan, sauté onions, celery,
   pepper, and garlic in olive oil until
   lightly browned.
2. Add remaining ingredients and, stirring
   constantly, bring to a light boil. Cover and
   let simmer for approximately 2 hours.

VARIATION
For Mushroom-Tomato Sauce, sauté 1 cup
sliced mushrooms with other vegetables.

TAHINI DRESSING
FOR GREEN SALADS

yield: 1 cup   preparation time: 5 minutes

½ cup olive oil
4 tablespoons tahini (sesame butter)
2 tablespoons lemon juice
2 garlic cloves, minced
salt and pepper to taste

Combine all ingredients in a blender and
blend well.

MAYONNAISE DRESSING

yield: ¼ cup   preparation time: 5 minutes

4 tablespoons mayonnaise
juice of ½ lemon
pinch each of mustard and curry powders
dash of tamari sauce
salt and pepper to taste

Blend all ingredients well and chill.
Pour over salads or cold vegetables.

FRENCH DRESSING

yield: ¾ cup   preparation time: 5 minutes

½ cup olive oil
¼ cup cider or tarragon vinegar
juice of ½ lemon
 1 garlic clove, pressed
½ teaspoon mustard powder
½ teaspoon tamari sauce
sugar to taste
salt and pepper to taste

Blend or shake all ingredients well and chill.
Pour over salads or cold vegetables.

NOTE

It might be convenient to make three or
four times the quantity of this recipe and store
it in a large bottle with a tight cover. It will
keep in the refrigerator for a long time.

BASIC CREAM SAUCE

yield: ¾ cup   preparation time: 10 minutes

2 tablespoons butter
2 tablespoons flour
½ cup milk or ¾ cup light sweet cream,
    at room temperature
salt and pepper to taste
pinch of nutmeg

1. Melt butter in a double boiler or small
   pan over low heat.
2. Add flour and stir constantly with a wooden
   spoon.
3. Gradually pour in milk or cream, stirring
   constantly, until mixture thickens. Sauce
   should be smooth—if lumpy, beat well with
   a beater. Season and serve hot.

NOTE

If a thinner sauce is desired, add more milk
or cream and stir well.

VARIATION

For a cheese sauce: Add ½ cup grated
Cheddar or combination Cheddar and
American cheese to sauce after adding milk.
Cheese should be thoroughly melted and
sauce smooth.

BROWN SAUCE

yield: 1½ cups   preparation time: 10 minutes

2 tablespoons butter or vegetable oil
1 small onion, chopped (optional)
2 tablespoons flour or arrowroot
1 cup boiling water
1 tablespoon or 1 envelope instant vegetable
  broth (preferably dark)
salt and pepper to taste
pinch each of thyme and ginger
1 tablespoon tamari sauce

1. In a small pan, melt butter and sauté
   onion (if used) lightly.
2. Over low heat, add flour and stir constantly
   with a wooden spoon until lightly browned.
3. Dissolve broth in boiling water and
   gradually pour into flour mixture. Continue
   stirring until mixture thickens. Sauce
   should be smooth; if lumpy, beat well with
   a beater.
4. Stir in seasoning and tamari sauce. Serve
   hot over vegetables, rice, grain, or pasta.

NOTE

Puréed vegetable soup or cooked vegetable
stock can be substituted for instant
vegetable broth.

MISO AND TAHINI SAUCE

yield: ¼ – ½ cup
preparation time: 10 minutes

1 tablespoon miso (soybean paste)
2 tablespoons tahini (sesame butter)
1 teaspoon grated orange peel
1 tablespoon arrowroot or flour
water

1. Blend miso and tahini together and add
   orange peel.
2. Over low heat, combine with arrowroot
   or flour; stir well until thickened.
3. Add water (amount of water will depend
   on consistency desired), blend well,
   and simmer. Serve hot or cold with
   vegetables or citrus fruits.

VARIATION

This sauce can be converted into a delicious
sandwich spread in the following manner:
Increase tahini to 4 tablespoons. Omit
arrowroot or flour, and add only 1 or 2
tablespoons water. Cook 5 minutes until
thickened. Cool and serve.

TAMARI AND TAHINI SAUCE

yield: ¼ cup   preparation time: 10 minutes

1 onion, chopped
1 teaspoon oil
1 tablespoon tamari sauce
1 tablespoon tahini (sesame butter)
arrowroot or flour (to thicken)
water

1. Sauté onion in oil until tender.
2. Blend tamari and tahini together and
   proceed as for Miso and Tahini Sauce
   (see above).
3. Serve hot with cooked vegetables.

chapter 9
DESSERTS AND BEVERAGES

Fruit is so full of vitamins that it has become a delicious necessity. Fruit, like vegetables, should be organically grown and free of sprays, preservatives and coloring. When in doubt, peel the skins.

The fruit desserts in this chapter include cooked or dried fruit; raw fruit should precede the meal.

It is necessary to give new thought to beverages; somehow most carbonated drinks, with their artificial colorings, sweeteners etc., seem out of place with this kind of food. I hope you will use the beverage recipes as suggestions and let your imagination be the only limit to the drinks you can create.

NUTTY PEACHES

servings: 4   preparation time: 15 minutes

4 large cooked peach halves
1 tablespoon butter, melted
½ cup chopped nuts
2 tablespoons sugar or honey
½ teaspoon cinnamon

1. Brush peach halves with butter.
2. Fill with nuts and sprinkle sugar or honey and cinnamon on top.
3. Broil about 3 inches from heat for 10 minutes.
4. Serve hot, with whipped cream if desired.

OLD-FASHIONED STEWED FRUIT

servings: 6–8   preparation time: 1 hour
                 (not including chilling)

2 cups water
1 cup sugar or honey
juice and pulp of 1 lemon
3 pounds fresh pears, peaches, or apricots

1. Boil water with sugar or honey and lemon until syrupy, approximately ½ hour
2. Peel fruit, cut in halves, and remove stones.
3. Cook fruit in syrup on medium heat for 15 minutes.
4. Chill and serve plain or with cream.

CZECHOSLOVAKIAN CRÊPES (POLATCHINKY)

yield: 6 large crêpes
preparation time: 30 minutes

  1 cup milk
  6 tablespoons flour
½ teaspoon sugar (optional)
  1 egg, beaten
½ teaspoon baking powder
  1 lemon rind, grated
pinch of salt
vegetable or seed oil

1. Combine all ingredients (except oil) and mix well.
2. Oil a frying pan very lightly and heat over medium heat.
3. Pour in 1 ladleful of batter and tilt pan until batter covers bottom entirely. Allow a thin layer of batter to adhere to bottom of pan and quickly pour the excess back into bowl. Prick with a knife while cooking, so that pancake will not rise. Cook quickly—approximately 2 minutes for each side—and remove crêpe to a warm plate. Repeat the process until all batter is used.
4. Spread crêpes with jam or nuts and cinnamon and roll or fold sides over into envelope shape. Serve warm.

APRICOT FREEZE

servings: 4   preparation time: 10 minutes
                     (not including freezing)

1 pound dried apricots, soaked until soft
1 cup honey
3 egg whites, stiffly beaten

1. Purée apricots and honey together in blender.
2. Fold in egg whites.
3. Pour into a greased mold or ice tray(s) and freeze. Serve frozen.

FRUIT DUMPLINGS

yield: about 25 dumplings
preparation time: 40 minutes

    3 medium potatoes, peeled and cut in
       large chunks
    2 eggs, beaten well
2¾ cups flour
salt to taste
    1 pound fresh apricots
    1 pound fresh plums
butter, softened
bread crumbs
cinnamon

1. Boil potaotes and mash with a little water
   and eggs.
2. Combine potato mixture with flour and
   salt. Beat into a smooth dough.
3. Roll dough until approximately ½ inch
   thick. Turn a large glass upside down,
   dip rim in flour, and, using rim, cut dough
   into circles.
4. Remove stones from fruits and fill each
   cavity with a scant teaspoon of sugar
   or honey.
5. Place a fruit in center of each circle
   and fold dough over fruit to make a ball.
   Roll between hands to smooth out.
6. Drop balls carefully into boiling salted
   water and cook until dumplings rise to
   surface, approximately 5 minutes.
7. Mix cinnamon with enough bread crumbs
   to cover dumplings. Roll dumplings gently
   first in bread crumbs and then in butter.
8. Place dumplings in a casserole and bake in
   a warm (350°) oven until browned. Serve
   hot, with or without a fruit sauce.

NOTE

Dumplings may be prepared in advance and
chilled, uncooked.

RHUBARB CRISP

servings: 4–6   preparation time: 1 hour

4 cups rhubarb, sliced small
½ cup orange juice
1 cup sugar or honey
1 tablespoon grated orange rind
1 tablespoon grated lemon rind
⅓ cup butter
2 cups coarse bread crumbs or Grain Cereal
  (see page 184).

1. Preheat oven to 350°.
2. Place rhubarb in greased baking dish and add orange juice.
3. Combine sugar or honey, orange, and lemon rinds. Sprinkle evenly over rhubarb.
4. Cut butter into bread crumbs or Grain Cereal with two knives until mixture is crumbly. Spread on top of rhubarb.
5. Bake for approximately 45 minutes, until rhubarb is tender. Serve hot or cold.

MILK AND HONEY

yield: 1 cup   preparation time: 5 minutes

1 cup milk
2 teaspoons honey
1 teaspoon butter
pinch each of powdered clove, nutmeg,
  and cinnamon

Combine all ingredients in a saucepan and heat through, but do not boil. Serve immediately.

NOTE

This is an excellent old-fashioned cold remedy.

YOGHURT AND APPLE DRINK

yield: 6 cups   preparation time: 5 minutes

  2 cups yoghurt
  2 cups apple juice
  2 cups water
¼ teaspoon cinnamon

Combine all ingredients and blend well.
Serve chilled.

NOTE

Fresh milk can be substituted for water for a
richer beverage.

VARIATION

Substitute 2 cups of any fruit yoghurt for
plain yoghurt, and use 2 cups of a compatible
fruit juice in place of apple juice. Omit
cinnamon, and add honey if desired.

RICE TEA

yield: 4 cups   preparation time: 25 minutes

½ cup rice
  4 cups water

1. Pan-toast rice over high heat, stirring
   constantly, until browned.
2. Add water, bring to a boil, and simmer
   for approximately 15 minutes.
3. Strain and serve.

NOTE

This tea can be chilled and served with
ice cubes.

VARIATION

Wheat berry can be substituted for rice.

MILK AND FRUIT DRINK

yield: 4 glasses   preparation time: 5 minutes

¼ cup powdered milk
 1 quart orange juice
 1 orange, peeled and cut
 1 tablespoon honey

Blend all ingredients with ice in a blender;
serve cold, with additional ice if desired.

VARIATIONS

Using a base of ¼ cup powdered milk,
blend the following.

Berries: Use 1 quart water, 1 cup fresh
berries, 1 tablespoon honey, 1 tablespoon
lemon juice, and a pinch of mint.

Apricots: Use 1 pound dried soaked apricots,
2 cups water (in which apricots were soaked),
2 cups any fruit juice, 1 tablespoon honey,
and a dash of vanilla.

Lemon-lime: Use the juice of ½ lemon and
2 limes, 3 cups water, and 4 tablespoons
honey.

Banana: Use 2 ripe bananas, 4 cups water,
1 teaspoon lemon juice, and 1 tablespoon
honey.

BASIC VEGETABLE JUICE COCKTAIL

yield: 5–6 cups   preparation time: 5 minutes

1 quart vegetable juice
1 cup water
2 tablespoons lemon juice
2 celery stalks, chopped fine
salt and pepper to taste

Combine all ingredients and purée well
in blender. Serve chilled.

chapter 10 POTPOURRI

This chapter includes those recipes which don't seem to fit into a specific category; also some sample meals you might want to try.

MAKE-YOUR-OWN YOGHURT

yield: 1 quart yoghurt
preparation time: 4 hours

1 quart milk
3 tablespoons powdered milk
1 package yoghurt culture or 3 tablespoons
  yoghurt

1. Combine milk and powdered milk in a pan
   and bring to a boil. Remove from heat,
   cover, and cool to lukewarm (about 115°).
2. Add yoghurt culture or yoghurt and stir
   very well. Pour into prewarmed clean
   jars. Cap jars and cover with towels to
   keep warm. Mixture must stay warm; place
   jars in warm water if necessary.
3. When mixture has thickened to desired
   consistency, refrigerate jars. Yoghurt is
   ready to use.

NOTE
For best results, use a high-quality milk and
culture (such as Bulgarian) or yoghurt.
Make succeeding batches—for up to a month
—by adding 3 tablespoons of this yoghurt
to milk mixture and repeating process.

SIMPLE FRUIT JAM

yield: 2 pounds   preparation time: 5 minutes
(not including soaking)

1 pound dried apricots, soaked until soft
1¼ pound honey
juice and rind of 1 lemon

Squeeze excess water from apricots and
purée all ingredients in a blender. Serve at
once or refrigerate in a tight jar or jars.

VARIATION

Other dried fruits or fresh strawberries may
be substituted for apricots—simply adjust
honey accordingly.

SHEPHERD'S BREAD*

yield: 6 slices   preparation time: 10 minutes

6 slices hard bread or rolls
water or milk
3 garlic cloves, cut in half
oil

Soak bread or rolls in water or milk to
soften. Fry garlic in oil until brown; add bread
and deep fry on both sides until crispy.

* So-called because it is a favorite dish
among shepherds and peasants in southern
Europe.

HOME-MADE GRAIN CEREAL

yield: 1½ pounds
preparation time: 30 minutes

 3 tablespoons butter or oil
¾ cup honey
 1 pound rolled oats
¾ cup sunflower seeds
½–¾ cups whole cashew, almonds, and/or
    hazelnuts
 1 cup wheat germ
¼ pound coconut, toasted (optional)
½ cup toasted sesame seeds
½ cup raisins
¼ cup other dried fruit, chopped

1. In a large pan, heat butter or oil and honey
   over medium heat. Add oats and stir
   until well coated with butter or oil.
2. When oats become golden, add sunflower
   seeds and nuts. Stir well and continue
   cooking.
3. When mixture begins to brown, add wheat
   germ and continue cooking for
   approximately 5 more minutes.
4. Add coconut (if used) and sesame seeds,
   stirring continuously for another 5 minutes.
   Mixture should be a rich brown.
5. Turn off heat, leave pan on stove, add
   fruit, and continue stirring for a few
   minutes.
6. Remove pan from stove and allow to cool.
   Store in a plastic bag or jar. Serve for
   breakfast, snacks, or as a dessert with
   yoghurt, milk, cream, honey, fresh fruit;
   or ice cream, etc., etc.

NOTE

This is an excellent substitute for bread
crumbs and may be used as a sweet
topping or wherever breading is needed.

NUTS, SEEDS, AND FRUITS

yield: your choice
preparation time: 3 minutes

sunflower seeds
roasted salted soybeans
almonds
cashews
raisins or currants
other dried fruit

Mix together and use as a delicious (and healthy) nibble.

HERB BUTTER

yield: ¼ cup   preparation time: 5 minutes

2 tablespoons butter
1 tablespoon oil
2 garlic cloves, pressed
1 tablespoon chopped oregano
1 tablespoon chopped basil
2 tablespoons grated Parmesan cheese
  (optional)

Blend all ingredients into a paste and chill for use on vegetables, pasta, bread, etc.

NOTE

Try to use fresh herbs. If those specified above are not available, others may be substituted.

SESAME SALT

yield: ¼ cup   preparation time: 20 minutes

8 tablespoons sesame seeds
1 tablespoon salt

1. Heat a large frying pan very hot.
2. Toast sesame seeds, stirring continuously with a wooden spoon, until lightly browned.
3. Place seeds and salt in a mortar and crush with a pestle until seeds are finely ground.
4. Return mixture to frying pan and stir over high heat until well browned.
5. Return to mortar and continue crushing mixture with pestle until it becomes a powder.
6. Store in a tight jar and use as a seasoning instead of salt; or as a topping for salad, soup, vegetables, etc.

NOTE

The proportion of eight parts seeds to one part salt is standard; for a saltier taste, it may be increased to six-to-one. Sesame salt should be prepared weekly, as it goes stale after that time. It must be kept dry.

SAMPLE MENUS

Here are some menus derived from recipes in this book:

1. Mixed Fruit Salad (see page 33).
   Artichoke and Egg in Mayonnaise
   (see page 28).
   Couscous with Vegetables (see page 120).
   Jelly Roll (see page 160).

2. Sweet Cream of Carrot Soup (see page 46).
   Eggs à la Russe (see page 58).
   Cuban Rice (see page 126).
   French Beans with Sunflower Seeds
   (see page 104).
   Fruit Dumplings (see page 174).

3. Cucumber and Yoghurt Salad
   (see page 25).
   All-Green-Vegetable Soup (see page 45).
   Middle Eastern Lima Beans (see page 137).
   Rice in Brown Sauce with Mushrooms
   (see page 168).
   Chapattis (see page 150).
   Apricot Freeze (see page 173).

4. Quick Cold Gazpacho (see page 51).
   Mushroom and Celery Appetizer
   (see page 143).
   Miguel's Authentic Spanish Omelette
   (see page 63).
   Fried Green Peppers (see page 85).
   Fruit and Nut Cake (see page 158).

INDEX